To: Nancy

What a Beautiful Sunset

Bless you,
Jim Hammond

What a Beautiful Sunset

by

James H. Hammond

What a Beautiful Sunset

ISBN 1-57399-372-7

© 2007 by James Herschel Hammond

Published by Mac Hammond Ministries

P.O. Box 29469
Minneapolis, MN 55429

Printed in the United States of America. All rights reserved under International Copyright Law. Contents and/or cover may not be reproduced in whole or in part in any form without the express written consent of the publisher.

Dedication

I dedicate this little story to Carey Willis Hammond, who was my beautiful and most beloved wife for 66 years before she departed this earth and went to heaven on March 10, 2006. I want my readers to know that *What A Beautiful Sunset* is not only a sequel to my autobiography, *A Kentucky Kernel & His Folks*, but it is as well a love story with Carey as my heroine.

It is with a heart filled to overflowing with love, devotion, admiration, and humility that I dedicate this book to my wonderful Carey. I thank God for bringing us together so long ago and for leading us through our long, happy marriage. I'm believing that a whole host of angels will celebrate and sing Hallelujah-Hallelujah-Hallelujah the day I join Carey in paradise.

About the Front Cover

Colonel Arnold (Arnie) W. Holcomb is like a member of my family. It would have been nice if I could have adopted him as my third grandson, but my two real ones were unwilling to share me.

Arnie's letter to me tells all about the beautiful sunset photo I used on the front cover of my "What a Beautiful Sunset" story.

To: Pops,
From: Arnie
When you mentioned "What a Beautiful Sunset," a photo I took with my camera in late July 2005 came to mind. I have attached it to this e-mail and you are welcome to use it if you wish. I took it from the Misawa Air Base golf course restaurant balcony overlooking Lake Ogawara. There were no filters or changes made to the coloring on the photo … what you see is natural color.
Love,
Arnie
Arnold W. Holcomb, Colonel, USAF
Commander, 376th Expeditionary Mission Support Group CENTAF, Manas Air Base, Kyrgyzstan

Additional Photos

The photo of the author on the back cover, as well as the picture on page 231, were taken by Rick Rickman in 2007 and are used by permission.

Contents

Chapter 1 • About Carey 1

Chapter 2 • 1995 69

Chapter 3 • 1996 79

Chapter 4 • 1997 87

Chapter 5 • 1998 103

Chapter 6 • 1999 109

Chapter 7 • 2000 115

Chapter 8 • 2001 121

Chapter 9 • 2002 133

Chapter 10 • 2003 143

Chapter 11 • 2004 161

Chapter 12 • 2005 173

Chapter 13 • 2006 179

Conclusion 229

Chapter 1

About Carey

Upon graduation from Georgia State College for Women in June 1936 with a Bachelor of Science degree in Biology, Carey enrolled in a one-year laboratory-technician training course at Emory University in Atlanta, Georgia. Concurrently and in conjunction with her studies at Emory University, she was given on-the-job training at Grady Hospital, Atlanta's famous charity hospital, as a part of her course at Emory. Upon its completion, she passed a state-required examination and became a duly certified and state-licensed laboratory technician, immediately following which she was employed by the State Board of Health in the Georgia State Health Department in the old capitol building in Atlanta.

Shortly after Carey went to work, destiny decreed that we meet for the first time on December 15, 1937. We fell madly in love almost immediately. All my life, my romantic soul had dreamed of falling "madly in love." However, since I had reached the ripe old age of 23 without once having experienced anything approaching such a powerful emotion, I had begun to despair, thinking something was wrong with me and that it had passed me by. Then, when least expected, there it was! WHAM BANG – I was hit like a bolt out of

What a Beautiful Sunset

the blue with more of it and far better than anything I had dreamed about all those years. After an eternity (two years and two weeks), we were married on December 31, 1939.

I brought to our marriage many rough edges while Carey brought only a few very small ones. Surprisingly soon, all of Carey's and almost all of mine had smoothed out and disappeared. Except for one of my very stubborn edges that took many years to be worn down, our personalities would have melded and become as one.

All my life I've loved to tell stories and if it took considerable embellishment to make them better, that's what I did and I did it well. To Carey, there was no such thing as a "white" lie. For her, the truth was the truth and an untruth was an untruth with no blurring in between. It was my nature to exaggerate if it made my story better and if it hurt no one.

She never hesitated to interrupt and correct my slightest embellishment, no matter how large or small my audience might have been. I can hear her now saying, "Jimmy, there were six of them, not eight." This both angered and embarrassed me but I never let it show until we got home. Then I'd let her have it. "Don't ever embarrass me like that again," I'd say and a lot more. She almost always ended up in tears and that I couldn't stand. I loved her too much to see her hurt and unhappy. It made me feel mean and heartless and I'd always be contrite and ask her to forgive me for the mean things I'd said. I would take her in my arms and love away her hurt and misery.

She always forgave me. The saving grace was that we always kissed and made up. Never once during our 66-year marriage did we go to sleep mad or unhappy. This scene

About Carey

was repeated many times down through the years but with diminishing frequency as my rough edge got filed down smoother and smoother. Even though it continued to be a work in progress, when we first reached our golden years, I do believe we had come closer to being "as one" than most couples ever come close to.

Carey never gave up and her determination to correct the character flaw that she abhorred never weakened. She would have called my hand when she was on her deathbed at the age of 91 if I had slipped up and shaded the truth in her presence. In our later years, she was much more tactful when she called my hand for shading the truth, as I know she appreciated my being mean to her no more when she did it.

I tried really hard to embellish nothing in my "What a Beautiful Sunset" story, but if any did slip in, it had to be small enough to slide under Carey's radar, as I heard no rumblings from heaven.

Despite her sweet, gentle, and southern-ladylike demeanor, Carey was very strong in the areas that really mattered. She was very smart too. She knew what she wanted most in life and she knew how to get it. What she wanted in life above all else was a really happy, fulfilling marriage and a Christian family in which each member loved and respected the others. She treated me as the head of our household, let me have my way in most things, make all business decisions and most family decisions as well, as long as not one of her moral principles was jeopardized; in which case, she stood as firmly as a rock that could not be budged.

When we married, we planned for Carey to continue working three or four years until we could afford to start our family. She loved her job, her fellow employees, and her boss, Dr. Sellers.

Our first home together was an apartment on West Peachtree Street at the intersection of 14th Street. Our apartment building was separated from West Peachtree Street by a sidewalk and six steps up to the entrance to our building. The hallway door to our second-floor apartment opened into a spacious living room with a bedroom and bath on the left and a small dinette and kitchen on the right. There was a Murphy bed for visiting friends and relatives that folded into the living-room wall – a wonderful space saver. I'm surprised that I've never seen one since. Our bedroom was on the front of the building. It was very close to and looked down upon West Peachtree Street. Each time a streetcar roared down West Peachtree Street and came to a screeching stop at 14th Street, our bedroom windows rattled and our bed vibrated, but we were too much in love to let the deafening streetcar noise or our vibrating bed bother us at all. To us, it was a small corner of paradise and we loved everything about it. It was ours.

I worked as Office Manager and assistant to the Regional Sales Manager at General Mills. My office was on Spring Street only four blocks from our apartment, so I walked to and from work every day.

Carey got home from work every day before I did. She always sat at our bedroom window and watched for me so she could be at our door to welcome me home with a big kiss. I felt very, very proud and manly to be the head of our household and of having a beautiful wife who always opened our door and welcomed me home with a kiss. She always bubbled with enthusiasm in her eagerness to share her day

About Carey

and have me share mine. I loved it when she followed me around as I shed my coat, shirt, and tie and changed into comfortable clothes, while she babbled on about her exciting day. Carey worked with a group of highly educated and very interesting people and she loved them all.

She had a wonderful and humorous way of describing her interactions with each of them that kept me entertained every evening. I felt that my days were far less interesting but she wanted to hear all of it. Coming home to Carey and our sharing time became the best and most enjoyable part of my day and continued to be throughout our marriage. The interest each of us had in the other's activities was a major ingredient in our happy-marriage recipe.

To know that I was totally enveloped by the joyous and unconditional love of someone like Carey was for me emotionally overwhelming. The emotional peaks and valleys smooth out with the passage of time and I suppose this is a good thing, as old folks need more peace and calm. However, to me, it's sad to know that never again can the unbridled intensity of young love be matched, except in one's memory.

For two years prior to our marriage, I ate lunch every day at a small restaurant near my office that served breakfast and lunch only and closed at 3 PM. I got to know and like a nice black lady named Mary who did double duty as cook and waitress. When I told her I was getting married, she asked me if my bride to be could cook. I told her she couldn't but was excited about learning. Since Carey planned to work until we started a family, Mary told me we needed someone to cook and clean and that she'd like to do it as she had plenty of time. The restaurant closed at 3 PM and it was a short walk to our apartment. When I asked her how much she'd charge and she told me $3 a week, Monday through Saturday, it was a done deal then and there.

Mary was absolutely incredible. She cleaned our apartment, did our laundry, grocery shopped, cooked our dinner, served it, and washed the dishes – all this for $3 a week, which was about the going rate for similar services at that time. There was a small Mom and Pop grocery store around the corner on 14th Street where Mary bought our groceries and charged them. We paid the bill every Saturday. She took great pride in keeping our bill low. She haggled with the store owner about prices on almost everything. Pork chops cost 15¢ each and several times she talked him into selling them for 10¢. She would gleefully tell us about it. The store owner told us she bickered over prices every day and it became a sort of game between them.

We realized much later how helpful Mary's services were in getting our young marriage off to a flying start in the right direction. We had none of the stresses that plague most young working couples. When they arrive home after a long day at work, there's still a lot of work ahead of them at home. For the first three years of our marriage, we were free as birds with plenty of energy to come and go as we pleased and do all the things we enjoyed as a couple. We had plenty of time without stress to make necessary adjustments that all newlyweds must make in order to live together happily.

Fortunately, we had few adjustments to make. We were alike in almost all respects. We liked the same people and enjoyed the same things. We had time to socialize and build friendships with other couples that have lasted a lifetime. A

About Carey

major thing in our favor was that we truly enjoyed and never grew tired of each other's company.

Of almost equal importance, neither of us had abrasive habits that irritated the other. For me, it was a wonderful thing to know that I could take her into any group with certain knowledge that she would be liked and found attractive. Unlike most young people, she was at ease with herself and happy with "who she was." Without a doubt, she was the most poised, natural, and unpretentious person I have ever known. She tried to impress no one. That's something that has taken me a long time to learn and I'm not sure I have really learned it yet, as I still find myself trying to impress someone now and then.

To get back to Mary, it was love at first sight with respect to her and Carey. Mary called her "Miss Carey Baby" and babied her as if she were one. I'll never forget our first dinner party shortly after we moved into our new apartment.

She invited two former boyfriends, Toby Tyler and Bob Bolen, both of whom I had met, for dinner. With Mary's help, she had our small dinette table beautifully decorated with a small flower arrangement and a new lace tablecloth. The table was set with her fine Chantilly (sterling) silver, Fostoria crystal water goblets, and her fine Havilland china. Everything on the table, except the flowers, was a wedding gift and she could hardly wait to use them.

When she told me she planned to use her silver hostess bell that was also a wedding gift, I told her it would be ridiculous, but she thought it would be fun and she was right. It was a lot of fun and Mary loved it. Since Mary's specialty was fried chicken and all southern boys loved fried chicken, that was her main dish. Carey was in her glory in her new role

What a Beautiful Sunset

as a hostess of a dinner party. She had no problem making those two old friends feel at ease and in the mood for a good time.

One small problem did come up when we were being seated at our small dinette table. Toby was six feet four inches tall and there was no room under the table for his long legs. Amid much laughter, Carey quickly, and with no embarrassment, solved the problem. She slid Bob's chair on the opposite side a few inches closer to my end of the table and then slightly angled Toby's chair toward her chair so Toby's feet could stick out on the opposite side of the table between her chair and Bob's. Of course, Carey had to keep her feet tucked under her chair so her shins wouldn't touch Toby's. I made a big production out of peeping under the table now and then to make sure they weren't rubbing shins.

To add to the hilarity, Carey would jingle her little hostess bell and Mary from the kitchen (four feet away) would say, "Yes, Miss Carey?" Carey would say, "Please pass the hot rolls again, Mary." More laughter – the exact response she knew she'd get.

Mary enjoyed our party as much as we did. After our guests left, she said to me, "Miss Carey sho do like to put on the dowg, don't she?" It was a wonderful evening and everyone had a great time but Carey most of all. It was no surprise to me that she soon gained a reputation as a great hostess, a reputation that followed her to the last big (47 guests) party she hosted, the one that turned out to be her farewell party—the day of her fatal fall that led to her death six weeks later.

Both Carey and I had always been very weight conscious. Carey was beautiful and buxom when I first met her and she

About Carey

maintained her near-perfect figure until about mid-way through age 81. I weighed 140 pounds when we married and my weight stayed between 140 and 145 pounds throughout my life except for one brief period when I was overweight. We lived in Charleston, SC from 1945 to 1947 and I absolutely loved that high-calorie, "low country" cooking.

I allowed myself to overindulge in all that good stuff. I, of course, gained weight, but I won't say how much. In 1947, we moved back to Atlanta. Soon thereafter, word got back to me that the lady next door had said to someone, "A little fat man has moved in next door." It took me three weeks of fasting to get back to 145 pounds and never again did I weigh more than that.

As stated above, Carey was beautiful and buxom when we married and I loved her perfect bust line, but I worried. I had always heard that buxom young girls become fat young ladies. I did not want my beautiful wife to be fat. Soon after we married, we spent a weekend with Carey's beloved aunt, Ethel ("Tutter") McBryde. Tutter was the best cook in the whole world. At Sunday dinner, Carey had her plate piled high with food and I clearly remember Tutter saying, "Mary Carey, you'd better watch what you eat. I do believe Jimmy will divorce you if you ever get fat." I'd never divorce her but I have to admit that the idea of a fat Carey was not at all appealing.

We had three wonderful, carefree years to get to know each other and to establish a firm foundation for a happy, lasting marriage before starting a family. I came from a large, happy family (seven children) and I wanted at least five and Carey was happy with that number. We had the RH Negative Factor before the medical world knew much about it or how to handle it. Having one child was no problem but one miscarriage after another followed for us—seven of them. Carey was afraid, despite my denials, that I would be unhappy with just one and kept trying.

Our only child, Mac, gave us such joy and total fulfillment that my desire for more died a natural death after about the third miscarriage. With just one, I was afraid she would tie him to her apron strings but she didn't. Instead, she taught him to be independent early on. She was a wonderful mother, and with her leadership, I became a pretty good dad. Mac has been hugely successful in the ministry and I like to think that his success had its roots in the way Carey and I, and especially Carey, brought him up. Carey's family was full of ministers and she was one happy lady the day he became one.

Since "What a Beautiful Sunset" is primarily a sequel to my autobiography, I do not plan to retell in narrative form my whole life story, so I'm going to do a fast-forward right here to 1996. I know it's a very long leap from the early days of our marriage in the early 40s to 1996, but I hope to bridge this gap for those who have not read my autobiography. Here's how. From this point forward to 1996, this will be a pictorial story. The following series of captioned, date-order photographs will tell our story and fill in the gap. After the pictures, Chapter 1 continues and depicts my life with Carey from 1996 until her death.

About Carey

Mary Carey Willis graduated from Georgia State College for Women (now Georgia College—a co-ed school) in June 1936 and this is her graduation picture. Wasn't she a doll!

What a Beautiful Sunset

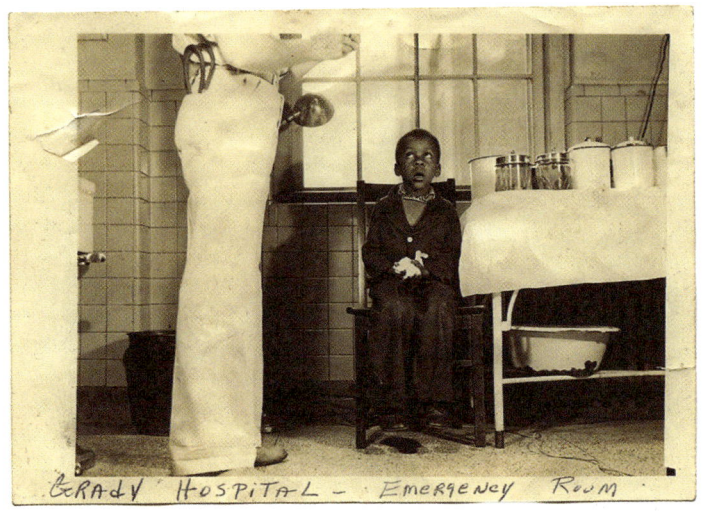

This picture was taken in 1938 in the emergency room at Atlanta's famous charity hospital, Grady Hospital, where Carey worked. To me, it's a classic picture.

Pattillo Villa where Carey and I, Johnny and Alice, Louise and Fred Fletcher, and many other couples met and married. It is still a show place.

Cupid Must Find New Hideout, Atlanta's Pattillo Villa Closing

By MARY KEY WYNNE.

Cupid must find another hideout by October 1. He has received official notice from Mrs. Ruth Pattillo.

Mrs. Pattillo, operator of Atlanta's Pattillo Villa at 1 Peachtree Circle, is giving up the boarding home which she has been running for 14 years. And with reluctance she is parting with the young business girls who have lived with her through the years.

"Cupid," said Mrs. Pattillo, "has been my active and constant competitor. But there's one nice thing about the fellow—though he usually takes two away, he always brings three back."

SETTING FOR WEDDING

"I guess the romance that clings around this place is what makes it so interesting. The stairway in the hall just suggests a beautiful wedding. Nearly every girl who has ever stayed here has some time remarked: 'This would be a lovely setting for a wedding.'"

Mrs. Pattillo, resting from the day's grind in an easy chair, recalled the many cases of "love at first sight" which she has seen blossom in her home. One such incident she remembered because of its unusual character.

"A girl by the name of Alice," she said, "was sent down from New York to work in the office of a nationally known magazine. A casual acquaintance on the train to Atlanta told her about the villa.

"The young girl came by to see me and it so happened that I had room for her. Now at the same time, Johnny, a newspaperman, also wanted a room. One of my girls had left me for a month so I let Johnny have her room for that time."

"IT WASN'T LONG"

"Well, Alice and Johnny met— and it was another case of love. They were both graceful dancers and did some entertaining at the Biltmore hotel.

"It wasn't so long until they were married. Now wasn't that an unusual affair? They were both journalists and dancing artists."

Pattillo Villa, affectionately named by the boys and girls who lived there, is a stately and majestic building. Inside the house, facing the stairway, one can picture it's more romantic days. Days when Mrs. Frank Ellis, former owner, staged elaborate and much-talked-about parties for famous opera stars who visited Atlanta.

The crystal chandeliers hanging from the high ceilings, the worn but fine carpets covering the floor, and the marble-topped tables give a hint of the more glorious days of Pattillo Villa. Yes, more glorious, but not happier days.

"FULL OF HAPPINESS"

According to Mrs. Pattillo, a devoted mother and grandmother, her home has always been full of happiness. "I keep a nice bunch of single boys and girls with me," she said. "I like them because they are so full of life, so gay."

That is the secret to Mrs. Pattillo's popularity as a landlady. She stays young with her guests. She takes only those who will fit into her scheme of a big, happy family.

The surroundings of her own room explain the personality of this perfect hostess. Round and about her private abode, are large, overstuffed chairs, what-nots filled with novelties significant only to her, heavy and handsomely-carved tables, and hand-painted pictures. These are relics of the past.

Then, there are the telephone, the radio, and the electric fan. These are the products of the present. She is a lady who holds to

Continued on next page

Continued from previous page

the fine and cultural things of bygone days, and a woman who readily accepts the modern life.

"CAN'T GET HELP"

Sentimental? Of course she is. "I don't see how I can stand to give up this place," she declared. "An accumulation of the memories of 14 years make it hard for me to leave, but I can't get the help necessary to run a guest house and the work is too much for me."

Then, there is the funny side of boarding house life at Patillo Villa. The genial lady told of the good old days when the boys were home. They stayed on the third floor, and taking a lot of pride in their penthouse, they decorated it to the "nth degree." The fellows named their floor "Blue Heaven."

"Now the girls didn't want to be outdone," Mrs. Pattillo laughed, "so they called Blue Heaven the 'Pant-House.'"

Mrs. Pattillo was in the Red Cross uniform all during the last World War, serving at Camp Gordon, Fort McPherson and in Key West. After her war duties were over, she opened the White Peacock tearoom in Washington, D. C.

PROMINENT PEOPLE CAME

"Why, all the prominent people came to the White Peacock—from congressmen to countesses," she smiled.

While Mrs. Pattillo was in Washington, she received an invitation from President and Mrs. Coolidge to visit the White House. She has that engraved invitation now. It is dated February 3, 1927.

After leaving Washington, Mrs. Pattillo opened the White Barn in Atlanta, and later moved to Pattillo Villa.

And now, with apologies to Cupid, the little man with the bow and heart-piercing arrows, Mrs. Ruth Pattillo will move to her new home at 95 The Prado.

This article appeared in the Atlanta Journal in 1943. The Johnny and Alice it refers to are Alice and Johnny Goodwin who have been our close friends for 70 years. They married December 31, 1937, two years to the day before Carey and I did.

Summer 1938. In this picture, Bill Jordan's date, Rose Lockhart, and I are standing in front of my first automobile, a 1934 Oldsmobile club coupe with a rumble seat. I still had this car when Carey and I married. The roof leaked so badly that we had to raise an umbrella when it rained.

About Carey

1938—My roommate, Bill Jordan, and his date, the brunette, on his right. My date, the beautiful blonde Rose Lockhart, is on Bill's left. Although we were never anything more than good friends, Rose Lockhart innocently came close to wrecking my romance with Carey—a misunderstanding that resulted in a 1½ year estrangement between Carey and me. During that time when I thought any hope for reconciliation was gone, I came close to choosing second best with a wonderful girl named Mary Williams who had marriage on her mind. I never stopped loving Carey and, thank goodness, I did wait for the reconciliation that did come at the end of that long year and a half.

This is a picture of Mary Williams and me.

What a Beautiful Sunset

Marriage of Miss Carey Willis And Mr. J. H. Hammond Announced

Announcement made by Mr. and Mrs. Carey C. Willis of Columbus of the marriage of their daughter, Mary Carey, to Mr. James Herschel Hammond of Franklin, Ky., and Atlanta, is of genuine interest to a wide circle of friends. The ceremony was performed by Dr. Louise D. Newton, pastor of Druid Hills Baptist church, December 31, 1939.

The bride wore an attractive dress of black faille and her corsage was of white roses, showered with lilies of the valley.

Mrs. Hammond is the daughter of Mr. Carey C. Willis and the late Mary Wesley Covinton. She is a graduate of the Columbus High School and received her Bachelor of Science degree from Georgia State College for Women, at Milledgeville. The last two years has been connected with the Georgia State Board of Health. She has been with the laboratory here since last May and has won scores of friends.

Mr. Hammond is the son of Dr. H. L. Hammond and the late Jimmie Estelle Bradshaw of Franklin, Ky. He was graduated from the Franklin High School and later attended the United States Naval Academy at Annapolis, Maryland. He is now connected with General Mills, Inc., in Atlanta.

Mrs. Hammond will join her husband in Atlanta at a later date.

About Carey

Carey and I after our wedding.

Pictured here are Louise and Fred Fletcher who were our only wedding attendants. They lived at the Pattillo Villa when we did. Like us, they met there and married a few months before we did.

What a Beautiful Sunset

This picture is part of General Mills' Southern Division Sales Department taken in 1939. I was the office manager for the sales department. The sales manager, Golden A. Pirkle, is seated in the front row, third from the left and I am seated next to him on his left.

This picture was taken in Atlanta in either 1940 or 1941 at the Henry Grady Hotel after a football game. From the front on the right are Alice Goodwin, Tippy Carnes, and Johnny Goodwin, and on the left, John Carnes, Carey, and I. Always a cut up, Johnny has a cheese straw under his nose.

About Carey

Carey and I living it up at the Hotel New Yorker while on our 1941 vacation. Carey is all decked out in expensive finery she borrowed from my more affluent sister, Nancy.

Easter, the black lady who is holding Mac, was born on a plantation in Talbot County, GA, owned by Uncle Bob McBryde's grandfather sometime around 1860. No one, including Easter, knew the exact year of her birth. Uncle Bob inherited the same 2,000 acre plantation on which Easter was born. She served as housekeeper and cook for Uncle Bob and Tutter until Uncle Bob died in 1950. He willed Easter the house on his land in which she had lived and included one acre of land that surrounded it. She lived there until her death shortly after Uncle Bob's. She was a wonderful person and was loved and treated like a family member.

What a Beautiful Sunset

Mac is in Uncle Bob's lap and Tutter is standing behind.

July 1944, Mac & Carey, Mac was 10 months old.

About Carey

Mac's first birthday picture taken on the balcony of our LaFayette Drive apartment in Ansley Park showing him digging into his birthday cake with both hands.

This picture of me was made in July 1944. I simply cannot believe I looked that young at the age of 30. I don't look old enough to shave but I'm sure I did.

What a Beautiful Sunset

Delta Traffic Office Headed By Hammond

James H. Hammond, Atlanta, has been promoted to city traffic manager of Delta Air Lines' ticket office at the Piedmont hotel, it was announced Tuesday.

A native of Kentucky, Mr. Hammond has been a resident of Atlanta since 1939. During World War II he served in the Naval Officer Procurement office here, and after his release in 1945 he was employed by Delta as traffic representative.

In February, 1946, Mr. Hammond was made manager of the line's Charleston, S. C., office, where he remained till his latest promotion.

JAMES HAMMOND

When I was a city sales manager for Delta Air Lines in Charleston, S.C. (1946-47), my office was located in the Francis Marion Hotel. There was a policeman named Mr. Johnson whose beat included the hotel and he spent a lot of time on that corner. Mac was fascinated with his gun and uniform and would stand in front of him and examine every detail of his outfit. They became great friends and we had to buy Mac a policeman uniform. He wore little else for a year and during that time we had to call him Mr. Johnson. If we called him Mac his response was always the same, "Don't call me Mac, I'm Mr. Johnson!".

SEPT. 1946 - 3 YRS. OLD

Charleston, S.C.

About Carey

Kentucky 1947—My grandmother "Granny Mat," Mac and I. Granny Mat, who was 88 years old at the time, died three years later.

This is our first little house on Skyland Drive in Brookhaven, a northern suburb of Atlanta. We bought it in 1948 for $7,900 and sold it two years later when we were transferred to Greensboro, NC, for $10,500.

What a Beautiful Sunset

Our house on Heathwood Road, Charlotte, NC, where we lived from July 1, 1953 to July 1, 1956.

1953—From right to left: myself, my secretary, Carol Moody, and her assistant.

About Carey

Allstate President and Chairman of the Board Calvin Fentress is pictured presenting to me a plaque in recognition of our top national sales performance in 1954. To my left are Regional Manager Bob Leys and Executive V. P. Jud Branch.

What a Beautiful Sunset

(News Staff Photo by Tom Franklin's—Franklin)

ALLSTATE INSURANCE executives are pictured here at a meeting last night of Charlotte regional representatives at the Mecklenburg Hotel. Left to right are James H. Hammond, sales manager of the Charlotte regional office; Robert Leys, resident manager; G. H. Bartlett, assistant vice president from the Southeastern zone, Atlanta, Ga.; and R. D. Eger, sales manager from the southeastern zone.

Silver Bowl To Hammond

Allstate Manager Given Award

James H. Hammond, sales manager of the Charlotte branch, Allstate Insurance Co., was awarded a silver bowl for his efforts in the Allstate President's Birthday Contest at a meeting last night at the Mecklenburg Hotel.

The contest is an annual event to honor the Allstate president, Calvin Fentress Jr., for his leadership.

The awarding of the bowl to Mr. Hammond is emblematic of the outstanding sales record set by the Charlotte Branch Regional Office in competition with 26 regional offices in the U. S. and Canada.

Grenell H. Bartlett, zone vice president, from Atlanta, made the presentation to Mr. Hammond, who, in accepting the award for his sales staff, expressed his personal thanks to "Mr. and Mrs. Allstate Agent" for their role in setting the sales record.

Also attending the Charlotte regional branch meeting were Robert D. Eger, zone sales manager from Atlanta, Robert Leys, Rodney Gabler, Richard J. Haayen, Royce V. Martin, Ernest R. Lemon, Thomas H. Cole, Eugene H. Percy, Hilton Borthen, Norman Carroll, Paul Wilkerson, Wylie Dawkins, Vernon Dalton, Walter Godwin, and Sara Berrier, all of Charlotte.

About Carey

In the summer of 1954, we held a Hammond family reunion at Nags Head Beach, NC. All my brothers and sisters and their families, except George and Jeanette, attended. Mac remembers it as our best vacation ever and, in recent years, has tried several times unsuccessfully to arouse enough interest in holding another reunion there. Due to its isolated location, transportation is a problem. Mac is pictured with his first cousin, Nancy Carol Bluett, my sister Evelyn's daughter.

My sister Nancy Murphy, her daughter, Martha, and her son, Jerry, who is now Dean of the Graduate School of Education at Harvard University.

What a Beautiful Sunset

1954. I'm addressing an Allstate Sales Conference in Charlotte.

1955. I'm addressing a large Allstate sales conference at Old Point Comfort, Virginia.

About Carey

After the Old Point Comfort Conference was over, we're in the parking lot doing our "goodbyes" before the Home Office executives headed back north to Chicago and I headed back south to Charlotte. I'm shaking the hand of Jud Branch, Executive V.P. and soon to be President and CEO of Allstate.

We moved from Charlotte, NC, to Roanoke, VA, on July 1, 1956 when I was promoted to Sales Manager of the Roanoke Region where I served until September 1, 1969, at which I was transferred to Allstate's Florida Region.

Allstate Promotes James H. Hammond

James H. Hammond has been promoted to sales manager of the Allstate Insurance Co.'s Roanoke Regional Office, it was announced yesterday by R. E. Coller, resident manager. He succeeds Roland G. Hagedorn, who has been transferred to the company's Florida branch as the public relations manager.

Hammond will supervise the sales force of the Roanoke office in the states of Virginia, West Virginia, Maryland and the District of Columbia.

A native of Franklin, Ky., Hammond joined Allstate as an agent in 1949 in Atlanta, Ga. He was promoted to district sales manager in 1950 in the Atlanta branch and in 1953 he was appointed sales manager of the Charlotte, N.C., branch office.

What a Beautiful Sunset

We bought this house on Timberlane Ave. in Roanoke, VA in July 1956 when we were transferred from Charlotte to Roanoke. This picture should support that I take my flower gardening hobby seriously.

Another photo from our home on Timberlane Ave. of my flower garden.

About Carey

This is a picture of my four sisters in order of their age. From left to right, beginning with Jeanette, my youngest sister, they are Jeanette, Nancy, Evelyn, and Laura. It was made in August 1956 following an afternoon tea at the Franklin Country Club which was given by my sister, Evelyn, in honor of my niece, Nancy Boyd Hammond, a bride-to-be. I prize this picture very highly as it is the only one ever made of all four of my beautiful sisters together.

Carey, Mac, and me with our dog Rufus in 1958.

What a Beautiful Sunset

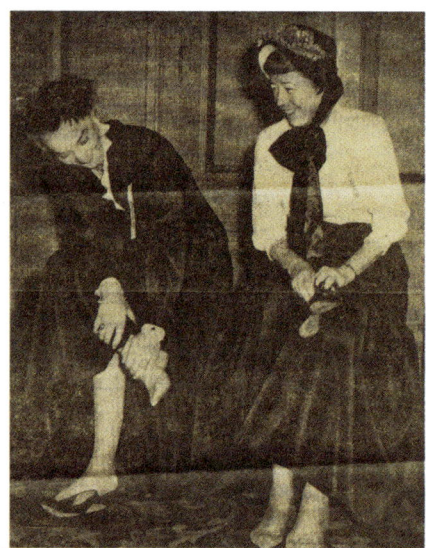

FEDERATED FATIGUE—Ushers and pages at the Virginia Federation of Women's Clubs convention in Roanoke find that their 1907 skirts provide a perfect hiding place for weary feet. Resting for a moment outside meeting-room doors are Mrs. H. J. Wilt, chairman of ushers and pages, and Mrs. James Hammond. Both are of Roanoke.
—Hazelgrove Photo

1962. Mac at field training camp during his second year at VMI.

About Carey

In 1964, John and Meredith Graves of Montgomery, Alabama sent their beautiful identical twin daughters, Lynne and Lucy, off to an all-girl college, Southern Seminary, in far-away Buna Vista, Virginia to protect them from all those wild University of Alabama boys. They didn't know that there were two all-male universities five miles from Buna Vista at Lexington, VA, Virginia Military Institute and Washington & Lee University. In early January 1965, Mac met Lynne on a blind date. The next day, Mac called his mother and said, "Mom, last night, I met the girl I'm going to marry." He was a senior and she was a freshman. Upon Mac's graduation from VMI in June that same year (1965), he was commissioned as a 2nd Lieutenant in the U. S. Air Force and sent to Moody Air Force Base in Valdosta, Georgia for pilot training. He and Lynne were married the following year on February 12, 1966. They are pictured in this series of photos in January 1965 shortly after their first date.

1965. Mac in VMI full dress uniform.

1965. Lynne.

1965. Mac & Lynne.

About Carey

Dogwood Lane, Roanoke

While still living on Timberlane, we bought a beautiful, heavily wooded lot on Dogwood Lane in a new subdivision called Jefferson Hills and contracted to have a house built to our specifications. Although we had previously bought new houses, this was our first experience building one from scratch. It was so much fun to watch and take part in every phase of its construction that we became addicted to building new houses. We did not know then that we would build four more dream houses. In order to extend my flower-growing hobby to a year-round activity, I had an attached greenhouse built with automatic heat, ventilation, misting, and humidity controls. We moved into our new home in the summer of 1964. Once again, I had the joy and excitement of landscaping and beautifying another yard, always striving to make the current one more beautiful than the last.

What a Beautiful Sunset

Mac entered the Virginia Military Institute, Lexington, VA, in the fall of 1961 as a "rat" and graduated as a 2nd Lieutenant in June 1965. He is pictured receiving his diploma. Astronaut John Glenn was the speaker at his commencement exercise.

About Carey

Miss Louise Lynne Graves

Miss Graves to Wed Lt. James Hammond

Mr. and Mrs. John Graves of Montgomery, Ala., announce the engagement of their daughter, Louise Lynne, to Lt. James McBryde Hammond, son of Mr. and Mrs. James H. Hammond of Roanoke.

The wedding is to be Feb. 12 in the Church of the Ascension in Montgomery.

★ ★

Miss Graves is a granddaughter of Mrs. Henry Ravesies Seawell and the late Mr. Seawell of Montgomery and of the late Mr. and Mrs. Henry Norman Graves.

She attends Southern Seminary and is a member of the Montgomery Cotillion Club. She was presented at the 1964 Blue-Gray Colonels Ball where she and her twin sister were queens of the ball.

★ ★

Mr. Hammond is a grandson of the late Mr. and Mrs. Carey C. Willis of Columbus, Ga., and the late Mr. and Mrs. Herschel Hammond of Franklin, Ky.

He was graduated from Virginia Military Institute and is now stationed at Moody Air Force Base, Valdosta, Ga.

What a Beautiful Sunset

14 Roanoke World-News, Saturday, February 26, 1966

Hammond-Graves Ceremony Held In Montgomery, Ala.

Miss Louise Lynne Graves and Lt. James McBryde Hammond were married Feb. 12 in a 6 p.m. ceremony in the Episcopal Church of the Ascension, Montgomery, Ala. The Rev. Mark Waldo officiated.

The bride is a daughter of Mr. and Mrs. John Graves of Montgomery. Parents of the bridegroom are Mr. and Mrs. James Herschel Hammond of Roanoke.

Given in marriage by her father, the bride wore a formal gown of candlelight delustered satin styled with a portrait neckline outlined in lace, long sleeves, and a flare front skirt. Panels of heavily pearled lace overlaid the demi-wateau train.

She wore a Brussels lace mantilla and carried a prayerbook with an orchid and stephanotis.

★ ★

Miss Lucy Graves, twin sister of the bride, was maid of honor. Bridesmaids were Miss Louise Seawell, Miss Carol Kennedy, Miss Margaret Day, Miss Kitty Shertzer and Miss Lannie Goodwyn of Montgomery, and Miss Virginia Caldwell of Richmond, Va.

Lt. Michael Anderson Williams of Roanoke served as usher as did Lt. Winston Huffman, Warrenton; Richard Schilling and William Douglas Thomas, Roanoke; Lt. Nathan Stephens Smith, Newport News; and Thomas Morrison Dickinson, Richmond.

The bridegroom's father served as best man. Acolytes were cousins of the bride, Leonard Henderson Seawell and Henry Ravesies Seawell III.

★ ★

A reception was held at the Blue Inn in Montgomery after which the couple left for a wedding trip to Calloway Gardens, Pine Mountain.

The bridegroom is a graduate of Virginia Military Institute, and the bride attended Southern Seminary.

They will make their home in Valdosta, Ga., where Lt. Hammond is in flight training at Moody Air Force Base.

Mrs. James McBryde Hammond
(Miss Louise Lynne Graves)

About Carey

Lovely Lynne (Graves), daughter of Meredith and John Graves, and James McBryde Hammond were married Saturday evening at the Episcopal Church of the Ascension. They are pictured here at the rehearsal party given Friday evening at the Montgomery Country Club. See details in the Whirl.

Mac received his Air Force pilot training at Moody Air Force Base, Valdosta, GA (1965-66) and this is a picture with his bride of a few months, Lynne. This day was when he got his wings, a very proud day in his and our lives.

What a Beautiful Sunset

Mac and Lynne the day he got his wings from pilot training.

Carey was a great hostess and she loved to entertain. In 1968, I took this picture of our guests at a dinner party for our next-door neighbors on each side of us when we lived on Dogwood Lane in Roanoke, VA. At left are Jane and Charlie Deibel, and on the right are Ozzie and Dollene Osburn. It's sad to note that I'm the only one of the group still living. They were wonderful friends and great neighbors whose company we thoroughly enjoyed. This picture brings back many wonderful memories of the fun and good times we had with these two couples. It was a very happy time in our lives.

In early January 1969, Carey and I joined about 30 of our fellow members of the Hidden Valley Country Club on a 17-day Caribbean cruise, our first of many cruises that followed in years to come. We left Roanoke in the middle of a huge snowstorm on a chartered bus for Norfolk where we boarded the New Amsterdam. Two days later we were basking in the warm Caribbean sunshine. We enjoyed it so much that it became our favorite mode of vacation travel. In the photo above, Carey and I are sitting with Hidden Valley friends.

What a Beautiful Sunset

This is our house in Juno Isles, the first of two houses we built in Florida. Mac and his family visited us in the summer of 1970.

We built a home on Point Manalapan on Land's End Road just one block from the golf course in 1972.

Our house on LaSalle Street in Baton Rouge, Louisiana, where we lived for two years, 1973-74.

About Carey

Good friends from Roanoke, VA who came for a visit and to play in a big duplicate bridge tournament. From left to right, Lillian Dillon, Carey, Minnie King Thomas, and Helen Weimer. It's sad that both Lillian and Helen died in recent years.

Carey in Baton Rouge home in 1973.

What a Beautiful Sunset

Baton Rouge agency force is pictured here helping me celebrate my 60th birthday.

My office staff celebrating my 60th birthday in 1974.

About Carey

1/1/75 - 2/1/79. Meridian, MS. About six months before my retirement from Allstate on January 1, 1975, while still living in Baton Rouge, I contracted to have a new home built in a beautiful new subdivision about five miles from the Meridian, Mississippi city limits. We moved to Meridian because that was where Mac and his family lived and where he owned and operated an aviation business. Our new house was completed on schedule and ready for our occupancy on January 1, 1975. It was a wonderful community with great neighbors and we thoroughly enjoyed living there until Mac and his family moved to Minneapolis in 1978 and we moved to Valdosta, Georgia on February 1, 1979. Here's a photo of our Meridian home.

Meridian—1978. Two of Carey's passions were duplicate bridge (life master) and flower arranging (National Flower Show Judge). When we bought our first little house on Skyland Drive in Brookhaven, a suburb of Atlanta, she joined a neighborhood garden club. At the time of the club's first flower show, two zinnias were the only flowers we had blooming in our yard. She stuck two zinnia blooms in a vase along

Continued on next page

45

What a Beautiful Sunset

Continued from previous page

with a couple of leaves and tried to hide it behind a large arrangement so nobody would notice it. However, the Judge did find it and said "I love the simplicity of this one" and gave it the blue ribbon. That set her on fire and she continued winning ribbons in almost every show she had ever entered. I don't understand the art. For example, the one pictured won top prize in a very large show but, to me, it's just a piece of wood with a skinny little vine climbing up it.

At the end of a year when my landscaping job was finished, I became restless and began looking for another interesting and challenging project. I found one that was more fun and more rewarding than any I had previously undertaken. I bought a pet shop in March 1980. Initially, I wasn't thinking in terms of a money-making business, but more or less as a hobby and a great sales outlet for the exotic birds I was already raising. To my amazement, it was profitable from the very beginning. Many small businesses fail because of insufficient working capital. I was blessed in this regard and never encountered a cash-flow problem as so many small businesses do. During the 13 years I owned and operated my pet shop, it grew and became hugely successful and a very profitable business venture.

About Carey

Those 13 years were among the most enjoyable and most satisfying years of my life. I'd still be operating that business today had my vision not deteriorated to the point that I could not distinguish between a five and a 50-dollar bill. More than once in making change for a customer I mistook a five for a fifty. Fortunately, most pet lovers are honest and they would inform me of my mistake. I named my business Wings Pet Shop and I became know as Mr. Wings or "the birdman." My shop is pictured here.

Wings Pet Shop 1992. Standing left to right, Judy Westberry, me, and my grandson, John. Seated left to right, Melissa Whitfield and Janice Bonner.

BUSINESS

Retirement Is For The Birds, At Least In Hammond's Case

By MICK HENDERSON
Times Staff Writer

Most people think of retirement as a time when you settle back and take it easy after working most of your life, but Jim Hammond, owner of Wing's Pet Shop and Grooming Salon here, has not found that to be the case.

"I just love it," he said of his present work. "It's just fun. I look forward to going to the shop."

After retiring from a career with Allstate Insurance in 1974, the 69-year-old Hammond has been involved in the breeding of birds and as of 1980 has sold them from the business in the Brookwood Plaza Shopping Center.

Although "it's a very demanding thing," he said he finds the retail business a challenge and is having the best time of his life.

Moving with his wife to Valdosta in 1979 after five years of traveling, he bought the shop, formerly Aquapets, in February of 1980, added the grooming shop last year, and in addition to birds, sells fish, puppies, kittens, hamsters, gerbils, rats, tarantulas and all kinds of pet supplies.

Of birds, he said, "it's just an interest that I developed real young," adding that his first fascination with them stemmed from collecting a series of cards depicting exotic species that used to be given away in boxes of Arm and Hammer baking soda.

That interest led him to a hobby of birdwatching, of looking for birds at zoos whenever he visited a city in his work and finally, after his retirement, to breeding baby cockatiels and parakeets.

The latter activity started in Meridian, Miss. with a dozen birds and has grown to a present flock of about 100 cockatiels and from 150 to 200 parakeets that he keeps in two birdhouses known as aviaries behind his residence in the subdivision of Wood Valley.

But his true love of birds is revealed by the fact that after selling the baby birds, he teaches others how to raise them as well.

"I can't tell you how many people I've started raising them," he said, remembering how one Valdosta State student bombarded him with calls when his two cockatiels were mating and starting a family.

"I walked him through that romance," he said, laughing. "It was practically like being a doctor."

Althought the baby birds need taming, he said he's discovered that by holding them against your body and rubbing their beaks, they can respond within as little as 30 minutes.

"Birds take strong likes and dislikes to people," he said. "They have to have total confidence in you."

They also have excellent memories, he said, relating the story of Oscar, an African Gray parrot at the shop who growls whenever Hammond is near, because he's never forgiven his owner for thumping him on the beak to cure him from biting over five years ago.

Hammond's point about total confidence was well demonstrated when he placed his finger in the mouth of "Joe," a large green-winged macaw, whose massive beak exerts about 500 pounds per square inch.

Unlike a lot of pet shops, Wing's has several of the large birds right out in the open on stands and to a first-time visitor it can be a bit disquieting.

But Hammond said the birds, including "Festus," a blue and green macaw who hangs from a chain on the ceiling and yells "help," and "Sunny," a sun conure who "likes people better than birds," though not for sale, are

About Carey

The Valdosta Daily Times

tame, great advertising and have a group of fans who come in regularly to visit with them.

Having the birds out in the open can be hazardous though, he said, and recalled the time "Festus" grabbed a woman's hair from behind while she was looking at the fish tanks and nearly scared her to death when she turned around and found herself almost nose-to-beak with him.

Usually only the males of each species of bird can be taught to speak by constant repetition, he said, and contrary to popular belief, they speak in response to certain situations instead of just at random.

"Maggie," a 2-year-old blue-front Amazon parrot which lives in his home, sounds exactly like his wife Carey, he said, and has him continually going up the stairs when he's in the basement with calls of "Jimmy" and says "mornin'" just like his wife does early in the morning when he comes down to breakfast.

Besides the birds themselves, another part of the pet shop business that has impressed him is the kind of people it attracts, he said.

"I just have great customers. I'm convinced that people who love pets are more honest," he said, adding that in nearly four years at the shop he has had only one bad check.

Prices for the talking birds range from around $50 for a cockatiel to as much as $2,500 for a magnificent white Moluccan cockatoo named "Duke" who's perched on a stand at the front of the store.

Hammond said at about fifteen minutes before closing time most days he never has to worry about customers being in the store, because the birds, as if they were expressing pent-up aggression from the day, start screaming in unison, but stop just as quickly when he locks the door to go home.

"It's deafening," he said, adding that he keeps a pair of earplugs handy just in case he needs to talk to one of his employees during that time.

What a Beautiful Sunset

The Valdosta Daily Times
Sunday, May 12, 1985

Move Proves Beneficial For Wings Shop, Salon

Owner, Operator Jim Hammond With One Of Many Feathered Friends

Times Staff Photo by Mick Henderson

By MICK HENDERSON
Times Staff Writer

According to owner Jim Hammond, the increase in business at his Wings Pet Shop and Grooming Salon since a recent move to The Marketplace expansion near North Ashley Street has been nothing short of phenomenal.

"The wonderful visibility is the main thing. I have an unbelievable number of people that have come in that didn't know there was a pet shop like this in town," he said, adding he considered the new location "ideal," especially because of its proximity to a constant flow of traffic on North Ashley.

The shop's location and size are undoubdetly a welcome change from its rather cramped former home off the center "alley" at Brookwood Plaza Shopping Center where Hammomd first established it in 1980.

He said he has roughly twice the amount of room as at the old location and consequently a much larger stock of pets and pet supplies.

Those pets include kittens, puppies, guinea pigs, gerbils, rabbits, mice, all kinds of tropical fish and as the business' name implies, all types of birds.

Birds hold a particular fascination for Hammond. A mainstay of the feathered population at the new shop as at the old are his talking parrots and macaws, many of whom sit on perches next to the large windows facing the sidewalks around the shop.

Enlivening the proceedings at the business are "Joe," a green-winged macaw, "Duke," a large white Moluccan cockatoo, "Festus," a blue and green macaw and his girlfriend "Baby", and "Lucy," a green African parrot who is the store's "main attraction," Hammond said.

On opening day March 21, Lucy greeted customers throughout the day with the phrase "praise the Lord!" and asked all those with food items "is it good?," Hammond said with a smile.

"A lot of people come in and tell me 'it looks loke a bloomin' jungle,'" he said with a grin. "They tell me they've been to pet shops all over and this is the nicest arrangement they've seen."

The business' grooming parlor, relegated to a crowded back room at the former location, has much more room at its new home and even its own seperate entrance featuring a striped awning and a miniature rotating barber shop pole.

With the added room and three experienced groomers manning the clippers, Hammond said business had about tripled in that area since the move.

He said the space was pretty much a shell inside when he first moved over and he designed everthing inside, including the enclosures that house the fish tanks and many of the animals that he made as maintenance-free and convenient for customers as possible.

What a Beautiful Sunset

Pets/A Feature About People And Their Pets

Sought-After Birds Nest In Valdosta

By JUDY SCHRAMM
Times Staff Writer

Jim Hammond says he's never had any problem attracting the "most sought after bird in America."

About five years ago, Hammond set up 40 man-made purple martin nests outside of Wing's Pet Shop, where he works.

Before the year was over, he had a colony of the small, shiny black birds with a purple tint roosting in the parking lot of the Ashley Street shopping center where the pet shop is located.

These birds migrate from South America during the summer, nesting in particular locations throughout the East Coast.

"You have to have the definite right house for them and they have to be placed right," Hammond said. "It can't be near a tree."

Although Hammond said he's enjoyed watching purple martin colonies since he was a boy and loves the chirping they make, the birds are beneficial to people.

"Each bird can eat up to 10,000 mosquitoes a day," Hammond said. "That's exactly what the books say."

A subscriber to *Nature Society News*, a publication for purple martin watchers, Hammond said he read a letter to the editor a few years ago, asking if these birds would come to populated areas such as shopping mall parking lots.

> 'You have to have the definite right house for them and they have to be placed right," Hammond said ... It can't be near a tree.'
>
> — Jim Hammond
> Wing's Pet Shop

Hammond immediately wrote in to tell the magazine's editors about his setup in Valdosta. He was then featured in an article in the national publication.

Because Hammond lives in a wooded area, he had to set up his nests at the store where there were no trees.

Atop four poles sits the gourds and purple martin houses which look like tiny doll house-size apartments. Each year about 40 pairs of purple martins travel from South America to roost in Hammond's nests, where they have offspring and then group together with other colonies for their migration south.

Hammond said he finds the birds particularly interesting because in January, one bird leaves each colony in South America and travels north to scout out summer dwellings. This bird then flies south, meeting the birds on their migration north, and leads them to various communities throughout the United States and Canada where they'll spend the summer.

About Carey

The bird feeders outside Wings Pet Shop at the Marketplace give a home to the sought-after martins — Times Photo by Paul Leavy.

What a Beautiful Sunset

Celebrating our 50th wedding anniversary (December 31, 1989) on a Caribbean cruise. Our good friends since 1937, Johnny and Alice Goodwin, accompanied us.

In the spring of 1991, we had a Hammond family reunion in Franklin, KY. My youngest sister, Jeanette, died one year later from pancreatic cancer. My sister Nancy and I are shown kissing her.

About Carey

At our reunion dinner, someone asked that Uncle James' favorite niece stand up. Eight of them stood. Two of the top contenders, Marcella on my right and Amy on left, are pictured here.

In November 1991, we took a two-week tour of New Zealand. It is the most beautiful country with the most spectacular scenery that we have ever visited. In this picture, our bus is stopped to allow a herd of sheep to cross the highway. This is what is known as a New Zealand traffic jam.

What a Beautiful Sunset

The North Island is similar to Scotland—beautiful green rolling hills covered with grazing sheep. It was their early spring when we were there. The South Island was completely different with its rugged spectacular beauty as illustrated by beautiful Medford Sound pictured here.

St. Augustine, FL 1992—Here I am with my namesake, James Hammond Agerholm. My niece Marcella's son. She knew when she gave her son my name she'd stay at or near the top of my list in the "Uncle James' Favorite Niece" competition.

About Carey

My 80th birthday dinner party was held on April 5, 1994, in Bowling Green, KY with 42 of my relatives attending. Pictured here is Mac cutting my birthday cake for me while I look on.

What a Beautiful Sunset

Celebrating my 80th birthday. This is four generation of James Hammonds with my great grandson, Jamey, being the youngest. Also included is my namesake, my grand nephew, James Hammond Agerholm.

About Carey

1991 family reunion in Kentucky. My sister Nancy is on my right and Jeanette on my left. Our old home place where we grew up can be seen in the background.

Mac and I standing on bridge that spans creek that runs in front of our house. Taken in 1994 when all of us were in Kentucky celebrating my 80th birthday. The trees around our house had been removed after 1991.

What a Beautiful Sunset

Sometime in early 1996, I noticed that Carey occasionally repeated herself and asked the same question more than once in a relatively short span of time. This was highly unusual for Carey as she had the sharpest mind and best memory of anyone I knew. She could play a hand of bridge and remember every card in it a week later. I knew something was drastically wrong when she forgot bridge club two times in a row.

I called Doctor Anderson, our family doctor and our good friend, and described her symptoms. He told me to bring her to his office right away. After talking to her and asking many questions, he told me he was sending her to a neurosurgeon as it appeared she might be in an early stage of Alzheimer's disease. I had suppressed a nagging fear that it might be that, but I was both terrified and devastated to have its likelihood confirmed.

It was totally out of character for Carey to be so submissive, not even asking why I was taking her to the doctor and asking no questions after we got there. She was a trained laboratory technician, had worked in hospitals and around doctors. I knew she was sharp enough to know from the doctor's questions that he was testing her memory. She had most likely already diagnosed her own case but was afraid to ask questions and confirm it.

She drove us to the neurosurgeon's office in total silence—still no questions. After numerous, lengthy tests, the neurosurgeon called me into his office. He told me that everything else had been ruled out so he had to assume that it was Alzheimer's in its early stage. He tried to prepare me for what lay ahead for her and for me. It was horrible. When I rejoined Carey, it tore my heart out when she looked at me with terror in her eyes and asked in a pleading voice, "Jimmy, it's Alzheimer's isn't it?" I answered with tears in my eyes, "No, Carey, it isn't Alzheimer's." In all her loving goodness, she forgave me for that little white lie. She knew the truth but she also knew I was loving her and that my heart was breaking.

We lived only a few blocks from the doctor's office. While she was driving that short distance, something happened and I'll never know exactly what it was. When we got home, peace had replaced the terror in her eyes, and she was totally calm. She acted as if that day's events had never occurred. I don't know how she did it, but in every way, she was the exact same happy, loving Carey that she was the day before and always had been.

She never mentioned that day and it was as if it had never been. Her happy, positive outlook on life never wavered and she continued to enjoy life to the fullest each day as it came, right on up to the day of her fatal fall ten years later. Our lives moved on with no changes in our activities. We continued to travel and do all the things we had always done.

Never again in the next ten years that she lived did the word "Alzheimer's" cross her lips. She knew her memory wasn't normal and joked about it but it didn't appear that it bothered her at all and I don't believe it did. She lived her life as naturally as if her memory had been perfect. I never understood how she could play a memory-challenging game like duplicate bridge when she couldn't keep track of the days of the week but she could. Top duplicate bridge players do not like to play with partners who are not as good or better than themselves. And yet, the top players in Valdosta

What a Beautiful Sunset

continued to seek Carey out as their partner right on up to the day of her fall.

I know now that the neurosurgeon gave me a worst-case scenario. Had I known then what I know now, I would have been spared the horror of those first few days. Her life never began to approach the dark picture he painted for me.

Carey's case did not follow the norm for Alzheimer's. By the end of the first three years, her memory had stabilized at a quite manageable level for both of us and never worsened. In the last couple of years of her life, her arthritic knee and her limited mobility were more of a problem than her memory. She was still a delightful person and, despite her poor, short-term memory, she could converse as intelligently and as interestingly as anyone I know, right up until her fatal fall. Her quick wit and good humor were incredible. Everybody loved her and enjoyed her company.

Carey was one gutsy little lady. Her love of life and zest for living ended only when her life did. She loved to be "on the go." She missed not one of my track meets no matter when or where they were. She was right there for every family gathering and every family vacation. Nothing stopped her—not her very painful knee or her limited mobility, and she never, ever complained.

In Carey's situation, most people would have long since given up and become invalids, but not Carey. Her indomitable spirit recognized no limitations, mental or physical. Her active and enthusiastic participation in all our activities and life in general never slackened. You will see as my story unfolds that we lived quite normal lives, for the most part, as if Carey's disabilities didn't exist. It will be hard for anyone to believe that the last ten years of our lives together

About Carey

were among our busiest, happiest, and most rewarding years. Carey was truly a unique and quite remarkable lady.

It was early in 1996 that we visited the doctors about her memory problem, but there were no apparent changes in her overall health and she continued all of her many activities without interruption. In August, she had a couple of dizzy spells so we went to our doctor and found that her blood pressure was alarmingly high—200/100. Always before, it had been well within the normal range. It was a problem she had to contend with the rest of her life. Fortunately, she was able to keep it under control with medication. It concerned me greatly that she slowed down not one bit. She eliminated nothing to accommodate her time-consuming chauffeuring duties for me. She simply squeezed me into her busy schedule.

At first, I believed her high blood pressure was brought on by her internalization and suppression of a deep-seated fear of Alzheimer's. Now, in retrospect, I am certain that was not the case. From the day we visited that neurosurgeon until the day she died, it was so obvious that she was always at peace with herself and the world. I know her kind of peace can only come from God. Her unwavering faith in her Lord and Savior was the only thing that made it possible for her to put that dreaded disease behind her, never give it another thought, and face life so calmly with nothing but love, joy, and total peace. She never complained about anything, was always happy, and enjoyed each day as it came.

I have never known anyone who enjoyed good food more than did Carey, and she was a real connoisseur when it came to fine food. I believe that is the reason she became such a fabulous cook. An hour after finishing a meal, she

What a Beautiful Sunset

began looking forward to the next one. She had an alarm clock in her belly that started growling exactly 15 minutes before mealtime. I believe it was a lifelong thing. I have a postcard she mailed to her daddy in 1923 when she was eight years old. She was visiting her aunt, "Tutter" McBryde, in Geneva, GA. It read as follows:

"Dear Daddy,

It rained hard here this morning. Did it rain hard there? The sun is out now and it is hot. I have to go find something to eat now. I'm hungry. Write me back. I love you.

Your baby,

Mary Carey"

I love that card. I can't read it without smiling and thinking, "That's my Carey."

Most people with such appetites would weigh 250 pounds or more by age 30, but Carey would never have let that happen. For one thing, her principal goals in life were to make me happy and to have a good marriage. But she didn't do it just for me. She took pride in her appearance, loved beautiful clothes, and I'm sure she took pleasure, as did I, in the fact that she always looked great in them.

She learned to enjoy small servings of all the different foods she loved but she NEVER overate. That was her method of weight control and it worked for her. But that weight-control method flew right out the window the day after our visit with that neurosurgeon. That was shortly after her 81st birthday when she weighed 116 pounds. When I questioned the abrupt change in her eating habits, she calmly but firmly said, "You can stay thin if you like but I'm 81 years old and I'm going to enjoy the rest of my life to the fullest extent

About Carey

possible and that includes eating as much of anything and everything I like, with no worry about the consequences. And there's nothing you can do about it."

As I've said before, Carey never made idle threats and it worked exactly like she said it was going to, and as she said, there was absolutely nothing I could do about it, but I tried. The Lord only knows how hard I tried.

She loved hot buttered rolls and could make the best. When, after eating a full meal, she took another hot-buttered roll, there was no way I could resist saying, "Carey, please don't eat another one of those rolls." Very simply stated, there was nothing I could do about it when, with an impish gleam in her eye, she'd eat that one plus one more. Sometimes when she would still be eating after I had finished, I would ask as tactfully as possible, "Carey, aren't you about through?" She would smile sweetly and say, "No, I'm not full yet."

Carey loved Baby Ruth candy bars. She bought them by the bag full and ate one almost every night just before bedtime. I knew this habit was bad for her and tried to break it by hiding them. Due to her memory problem, she quite often lost things and depended on me to find them for her. Not so with the candy bars. She never stopped looking until she found them. When she did, she would hold one up and gleefully say, "You thought I wouldn't find them, didn't you?" It took me at least a year to relax and let her eat as much as she wanted to without badgering her. When I did, I think I might have beaten her at her own game. I believe it had become a game with her and she missed the fun of taunting me. At any rate, she began eating a little less.

What a Beautiful Sunset

My motive for doing everything I could to get her to eat less was twofold. I knew it was bad for her health and I did not want her to be fat. Of course, she did gain weight that first year and had to buy a whole new wardrobe, but she loved that. She was never happier than when shopping for new clothes. She never thought of herself as being fat, and she really wasn't—just a somewhat expanded girth and a bit hefty. She did look very nice in her new clothes despite the loss of her waistline.

Although she continued to eat heartily, her weight stabilized by the end of that first year and she remained about the same size. I became accustomed to her new size and was completely comfortable with it. Of all the ladies in their 80s, she was still the prettiest one to me. Thank heaven, that ended a quite trying time for me and we resumed our lives with almost no contention about anything. In retrospect, I know now this would not have been possible had I not learned two very hard lessons early on with respect to my response to her memory problem.

At first, I found it close to impossible to be patient when she asked me the same question more than once in a matter of moments. Too often, my response was, "Carey, that's the third time you've asked that question in the last 10 minutes." This always upset her and it upset me to see her upset. In addition, it made me feel both mean and guilty as I knew very well that she could not help it. It was almost as much out of my own self-interest as it was out of kindness to her that I forced myself to patiently answer the same question each time she asked it. Practice makes perfect and it didn't take too long for me to feel no impatience or irritation when I did it.

About Carey

The second hard lesson I had to learn was much harder for me than the first. Thankfully, the problem came up far less frequently. Sometimes Carey would stand me down that I had not told her something she considered important when I knew I had. It's my nature to argue until the cows come home when I know I'm right and Carey hated arguing throughout her life. It hurts now to know that I didn't avoid those unpleasant conflicts when I could have so easily done so if I had exercised a little self-discipline. But it helps to know that those brief and infrequent conflicts did little or nothing to deter her determination to enjoy life to the fullest. Eventually, I learned how to handle it. All I had to say was, "I'm sorry Carey. I fully intended to tell you but I forgot," and she happily accepted that with no further recriminations. Nevertheless, it never became easy for me and I had to fight the temptation to argue right to the end. Due to its infrequency, it never became a problem I couldn't handle. Through prayer and with God's help, those problems did not affect the quality of life for either of us. Otherwise, it is not likely that I could honestly say that those last years together left me with nothing but happy memories.

I believe this long chapter about Carey, that includes the details of her memory problem, undergirds and gives added significance to my story as told in the subsequent sequel chapters. It makes our incredibly good lives during the last ten years of her life, that encompass the time-frame of her memory loss, even more incredible. I also believe it forms a good platform from which to launch the sequel. It now begins where my autobiography ended.

Chapter 2

1995

When I completed my autobiography in October 1996 and it was published in April 1997, I was 83 years old. I thought that was a good age to end it as I anticipated little or nothing more exciting in my future than a very pleasant and peaceful stroll into the sunset. If I could have had a clairvoyant vision of my life for the rest of my 80s and on into my 90s, I would never have believed that so much fun and excitement could be possible for anyone at that stage in life. After having lived through it to the age of 92 and knowing that it really did happen, I felt compelled to write this sequel and tell the rest of my story.

You may wonder how I can remember all the many activities and events we experienced over this 10-year period, along with the exact date of each. I would like to impress you with what might appear to be my remarkable memory, but I cannot. That honest spirit of Carey's kept tugging at my sleeve to remind me to tell it like it was, so here's my confession.

When we first married, Carey accepted full responsibility for the writing of Christmas letters and notes to each and every one on our long list of friends and relatives. It was

What a Beautiful Sunset

a responsibility she retained for 53 years. She was a gifted writer, enjoyed it, and never skipped or dropped anyone. Folks used to say that a letter from Carey was like a really good visit. We lived in many different states and even more different cities and she made three or four really close friends in every place we ever lived. Carey's good friends were her friends for life, and through her, they became lifelong friends of mine as well. It was nice that she and I always chose the same couples as our best friends. If she liked them, so did I, and vice versa. There are many friends we haven't seen for years but those friendships have been maintained through phone calls and Carey's good letters.

When I retired for the second and final time in 1993, Carey decided it was also time for her to retire from her letter-writing job. I happily assumed that responsibility as I enjoy writing letters, I had time to do it, and I did not want to lose touch with any of our friends, no matter how long since we'd seen them. When Carey retired, it was for real. She never again wrote a letter, not even a thank you note. I did it all.

Each year since then, I have written lengthy Christmas letters (I don't know how to write short ones) telling our story for that year in terms of our travels, other events, activities, and experiences. We always eagerly check our mailbox beginning in early December as it always held several wonderful Christmas letters from friends and/or relatives from all across the country. It's sad that at age 92, I have outlived every one of my good friends from my pre-marriage and early-marriage days. One would think that my Christmas-letter list would now be short but it isn't. Our lost loved ones were replaced on the list by new friends we

1995

picked up along the way. Last Christmas, we mailed out 154 copies of my letter and I expect to mail about the same number again this year.

It is such a blessing that I stored copies of my annual Christmas letters in my computer Christmas-letter file. That file is a treasure chest filled with complete and accurate information about our lives for the past 10 years, without which I would be hard pressed to write this story. Now, it should be quick and easy. I'm proud that I responded to Carey's spirit and didn't try to impress you with my remarkable memory. It's all right there in black and white. Had I not resisted temptation, the rumbling sound from heaven might have been loud enough for all to hear. Now, on with my story...

On January 1, 1995, we were on board a cruise ship touring the Hawaiian Islands. Our 55th wedding anniversary was on December 31, 1994, and this was our anniversary cruise. Our good Valdosta friends, Rudy and Myrtis Howell, joined us on this trip and they were great traveling companions. Myrtis was one of Carey's favorite duplicate bridge partners. We flew to Honolulu on December 30 and boarded the cruise ship two days later and flew back home on January 10. It is a very romantic place but Carey did NOT come home pregnant.

For me, one of the most enjoyable events of that year was the celebration of Carey's 80th birthday on February 6, 1995. We had a Sunday buffet luncheon for 72 of our good Valdosta friends. Everybody raved about how great Carey looked and I have to say that I had never seen a more beautiful 80-year-old lady, and what a figure! Her new form-fitting dress showed it off to perfection and she

What a Beautiful Sunset

looked absolutely stunning. She weighed 112 pounds when we married and only 116 pounds at age 80. I was so proud of her I could hardly contain myself.

It wasn't all a bed of roses for me in 1995. My eye problem (macular degeneration) had worsened to the point that I was legally blind. I could no longer read or drive. It was devastating at first, especially not being able to read or drive, but our wonderful friends, and especially Carey, made certain I never lacked for transportation. The library for the visually impaired had a wonderful selection of books on tape, both fiction and non-fiction, that I thoroughly enjoyed. The only problem was, the readers had such soothing and melodious voices that I frequently dozed off and had to do a lot of rewinding.

I was blessed in that my peripheral vision was not impaired, and still isn't, and I could see almost everything except when looking straight ahead. The disease destroyed my central vision, without which one can't read or see fine details. I couldn't then and still can't see a person's features without getting right up in his or her face. That's not all bad when a pretty girl is involved. I'm too old to get slapped. I didn't then and still have no problem whatever getting about on foot or bumping into things.

Carey was most generous in her efforts to fit her duties as my personal chauffeur into her busy schedule and never complained.

After 70 years of sitting nowhere but in the driver's seat, shifting to the front seat on the passenger side was not a pleasant experience. I thought I was doing a fine job of back-seat driving from up front until the day Carey pulled to the side of the road, stopped the car, turned off the ignition switch, turned, looked me squarely in the eye and in a cool, calm voice, she said, "If you ever again criticize my driving, you'll find yourself on the side of the road thumbing your way home. Understand?" That brought my back-seat driving career to a screeching halt and an abrupt end. I had no choice. Carey made no idle threats and I knew she would do it. I think in her mind it was related to her "never lie" principle.

When she knew by the look in my eyes that she'd accomplished her mission, she started the car, drove off with a satisfied smile on her pretty face and instantly reverted to the sweet, gentle, and loving person she had previously been. Never again (in her presence) did I have the nerve to discuss her driving skills or rather the lack thereof.

To help make my life easier and more interesting at that point, I bought a new high-tech computer that could do wondrous things. I knew I'd never be able to master all of its capabilities but I felt that my efforts to do so might stimulate my mind and decelerate its rate of deterioration. I do believe it kept my mind much sharper than it would otherwise be. Despite my loss of vision and my inability to drive, I continued to attend Rotary every Wednesday, work at the soup kitchen, attend church every Sunday, and workout at the "Y" almost every day. I had books on tape to listen to and my new computer to play with. There was no time to feel sorry for myself or brood over my poor vision.

During that first year, I learned how to cope with my blindness in such a way that I had to curtail none of my activities other than driving and playing bridge. We continued to travel and we did not alter any of our other activities one iota. I was happy to learn that life could still be beautiful—some-

What a Beautiful Sunset

thing that seemed impossible initially. I began to notice how few people in their 80s, and even those in their 70s, could match my near-perfect health. It made me more acutely aware of how blessed I was and still am.

At age 80, Carey was as healthy as a horse, constantly on the go and, at that point, appeared to be indestructible. She was a garden clubber, flower arranger, a national flower show judge, a life-master duplicate bridge player, church worker, and a housekeeper. She was a marvelous cook, had always loved to entertain, and she still hosted a few small dinner parties, and she did it with ease and grace. She was a charming hostess and I was very proud of her. I marveled at and was amazed by her boundless energy. At her age, it was incredible to me. She was really something!

Here are some of our activities after I was pronounced legally blind in early 1995:

In April, I attended my old World War Two Navy Unit's reunion in Atlanta. It was sad to see how fast the ranks were dwindling.

We were in Atlanta from May 11th to the 14th for pre-wedding festivities and marriage of Grandson John to sweet Beckey Brown. It evolved into a Hammond family reunion with relatives from all over attending. I love weddings and family reunions. This combination was absolutely great. Lots of hugging, kissing, and loving going on—right up my alley!

In July, a fun younger couple from Mobile (we met them on our January Hawaiian Islands cruise) joined us on a two-week land and cruise-ship tour of Alaska. It was a fabulous trip! Most spectacular scenery we had seen since our trip to New Zealand two years before.

In mid-October, we spent a week in Minneapolis with Mac and our whole family. We loved being with all of them, but spending time with our two-year-old great grandson, Jamey, the fourth James Hammond, was an extra-special treat for both Carey and me.

In November, we went on a 10-day Caribbean cruise with John and Alice Goodwin of Richmond, VA, our best friends for 58 years. They were also with us on our 50th anniversary cruise in 1989. This was our third great cruise that year. That cruise was a wonderful way to round out our year. A pretty busy year for an 80-year-old lady and her 81-year-old blind husband, wouldn't you say?

What a Beautiful Sunset

In celebration of our 56th wedding anniversary on December 31, 1994, we flew to Honolulu and took an eight-day cruise of the Hawaiian Islands. Friends from Valdosta, Rudy and Myrtis Howell, went with us.

1995

This picture was taken following my grandson John's wedding on May 13, 1995. I'm on the left and following me from left to right are Carey, Mac, Carey's sister-in-law Jane Willis, Carey's brother Ed Willis, John, Beckey, and Lynne.

We took a helicopter flight to the top of a glacier while in Alaska. Quite an experience and we loved it.

What a Beautiful Sunset

In November 1995, we joined our old friends from the Patillo Villa days back in 1937, Alice & Johnny Goodwin, on a 7-day Caribbean cruise. Nineteen ninety-five was a busy and eventful year for us. Our 8-day 55th anniversary cruise of the Hawaiian Island began on December 31, 1994 and ended January 7, 1995, then our 7-day Caribbean cruise with our Charleston friends from April 21-28, next grandson John's wedding on May 13 and attended three days of wedding festivities, then in July, a 6-day land tour and 7-day cruise ship tour of Alaska and, finally, a 7-day Caribbean cruise with Alice & Johnny in November. This is a picture of us with Alice & Johnny in the dining room.

Chapter 3

1996

Last year (1995), Mac spent the week after Christmas in Valdosta, Georgia, with us. I have a big box filled with family documents (wills, letters, pictures, etc.), some of which date back to Revolutionary War days. They had been passed down to me by my maternal grandmother, Martha Isabella Boyd Bradshaw, my Granny Mat. When Mac asked about some ancestor, I opened up the box and we were digging through it and came across an old will made by James Herndon in 1808.

James Herndon was my great, great, great, great, great (5 greats) grandfather. He fought in the Revolutionary War as a Captain in the North Carolina Calvary. After the war, in 1792, he was given a land grant and moved his family to Logan County, Kentucky, where he prospered greatly. As other pioneer settlers became restless and moved farther west, he bought up their land grants, and after a few years, he owned more than 2,000 acres of debt-free, fertile, Kentucky farmland.

He built a huge plantation home. It was still standing and occupied during the Civil War by one of his direct descendants. My grandmother, Granny Mat, inherited a small portion of that original 1792 land grant.

What a Beautiful Sunset

I wish I had made a record of the many stories Granny Mat told me about the old days. I now remember only one. It seems that one of our ancestors, who fought in the Confederate Army, was captured and put in a Yankee prison camp in Indiana. Shortly before the war ended, he escaped and ran all the way to his plantation home in southern Kentucky. When he arrived, he said, "It was a long but pleasant run. Thereafter, that community was called "Pleasant Run." Could it be that I inherited my running genes from that ancestor? I was born on Granny Mat's farm in the Pleasant Run Community of Logan County, Kentucky and attended the one-room Pleasant Run School through the fourth grade.

I recently completed an 11-volume photo scrapbook history of the Hammond family entitled, *A Pleasant Run*. It is presented in date-order chapters with supporting photos and/or scrapbook items at the end of each chapter. It begins in the mid-1800s and ends in 2006. Each volume is beautifully bound with interesting pictures on each cover. My good friend, Russ Lofgren, Jr., who is a computer guru and graphic artist, is scanning every picture in this huge collection and digitalizing them (whatever that means) to enhance the clarity and quality of old, faded pictures and documents. He will then put the whole production on a CD (two if necessary) for distribution to members of my family.

Although I am very proud of it, *A Pleasant Run* is for family only as mass production would be much too expensive and, I suspect, of little interest to anyone other than family. I got sidetracked by *A Pleasant Run* as it was not a planned inclusion. It just occurred to me that if any of my descendants should read all three—*A Kentucky Kernel & His*

1996

Folks, A Pleasant Run and this one, *What A Beautiful Sunset*, they will certainly get a belly full of me and all our many ancestors.

In looking back, I wonder how I found enough hours in the day to complete these three time-consuming projects when considering all the many other activities in which we were involved. I think the answer lies in the fact that I sleep very little from the time I begin an interesting and exciting project until it is finished. I do most of my clearest thinking and get my best ideas when I'm in bed where I'm supposed to be sleeping. I keep a note pad on my bedside table as I know those great ideas will vanish by morning without notes to jog my memory. But making handwritten notes is not easy for someone legally blind like me. It is like writing with your eyes closed. A lot of time is wasted deciphering such notes. However, it is better than no notes at all. Thankfully, I have no such problem with typing. It's such a blessing that I learned to type without visual reference to the keyboard long before I lost my vision. Having done so much of it, I am now a speedy and quite accurate typist. Without my typing skill, I would not have been able to have completed any of these three stories as all were written after I lost my vision.

Now, I'll get back on track where I left Mac digging through that box full of old family documents. He was totally fascinated, especially by James Herndon's 1808 will. He said, "Dad, why don't you write your life story and our family history? If you don't, all this interesting family history, and our part in it, will be lost and gone forever and that would be a terrible shame."

What a Beautiful Sunset

The idea instantly appealed to me and I wondered why it had never occurred to me. I have always been interested in our family history. Mac urged me to start immediately and not procrastinate. He left on December 28 and I began writing on December 29, 1995, and wrote almost nonstop until *A Kentucky Kernel & His Folks* was finished on October 14, 1996—10 months and 16 days later.

Preoccupation with the writing of my book curtailed our travels in 1996. However, we did enjoy a wonderful Caribbean cruise with three couples, friends of ours from the two years we lived in Charleston, SC, way back in the 40s (1945-47). You'll read more about this cruise and a lot more about two of those friends, Sybil Mashburn and Gracelee Quillian, in the latter part of my story.

In July, we spent a week at beautiful Pelican Lake in northern Minnesota with Mac and his whole family. The temperature was in the mid-90s when we left Georgia, whereas we sat in front of a roaring fire to keep warm most nights at the lake. We loved being with all the children. Lots of fun. This trip to Minnesota was extra special for Carey and me because, for the first time, we met and spent time with our beautiful two-month-old second great grandson, Jessey Graves Hammond, John and Beckey's first born—a wonderful addition to our growing family.

Our family continued to grow when on October 8,1996, Hayden Hammond, our third great grandchild and our first great granddaughter joined the Hammond clan. We met her for the first time when we spent Thanksgiving week with the family. While Kristin and Baby Hayden were still in the hospital, Jim took three-year-old Jamey to see his baby sister for the first time. After looking her over very carefully, he said, "Good job, Mom."

We returned to Valdosta on November 30 and left the next day, December 1, for a one-week trip to Branson, Missouri, where we enjoyed all the beautiful Christmas musical shows—10 different ones.

Grandson Jim and wife Kristin

What a Beautiful Sunset

Grandson John and wife Beckey

First great grandson, Jamey, and his mother, Kristin

1996

We lived in Charleston, SC, for two years right after the war (1945-47). Among our closest friends while there were three couples, Grace & Gene Quillian, Bill & Nelie Thomas, and Charlie & Sybil Mashburn. After we left Charleston, we kept in touch with Charlie & Sybil (they lived in Atlanta) but we lost track of the other two couples. In February 1996, I came across a picture of Grace Quillian and, on the spur of the moment, I called to see if they still lived in Charleston. They did and so did Bill & Nelie Thomas; in fact, they lived next door to each other. Grace said to me that they, the Thomases and Mashburns, were going on a Caribbean cruise on April 21 and asked us to join them and we did. Grace suggested we surprise Charlie & Sybil. When we boarded the ship and went to dinner the first night, I heard Sybil say as we approached the dinner table, "That man looks exactly like Jim Hammond." As we got closer, she screamed, "It is Jim Hammond!" It was a wonderful reunion. It had been almost 50 years since we had seen the two Charleston couples but we took up right where we had left off and all of us agreed that it was our best cruise ever.

Seated from left to right: Gene and Grace Quillian, Charlie and Sybil Mashburn; standing left to right, myself, Carey, and Bill and Nelie Thomas.

What a Beautiful Sunset

Our granddaughter, LucyHart Hammond, was married on our 57th wedding anniversary, December 31, 1996, to Micheal Minton.

LucyHart and Micheal's wedding at Mac and Lynne's home in 1996.

Chapter 4

1997

The opening paragraph of my 1997 Christmas letter read as follows: "Without a doubt, 1997 has been the fastest moving, most exciting, and most rewarding one of my 83 years, as well as one of the most eventful."

When I reviewed the opening paragraph of the rest of my Christmas letters, I was amazed to find that in almost all of them I had said the same thing in a variety of ways. Now in retrospect, almost 10 years later, that assessment of 1997 still holds true. There were many great years before and after, but I do believe 1997 comes close to topping all of them.

In January, I bought a new high-tech machine called the "Magnum Magnifier." It enabled me to read printed material no matter how small the print. For me, that was a major breakthrough. It's like a color TV with a 21-inch screen that's mounted above a moveable platform on which reading material is placed. The print can be enlarged to a readable size and projected onto the screen. Once again, I could handle our financial affairs and do such things as write checks, pay bills, and even balance our checkbook. I felt handicapped hardly at all. Carey was equally elated as she hated the responsibility of handling our finances.

What a Beautiful Sunset

My book went to the printers in January and it was published in April. That's when the fireworks and excitement began and, for me, it was like the fourth of July for the balance of the year and on into early 1998.

I immediately took a copy of my book to a lady at *The Valdosta Daily Times* who did a weekly book review and asked her to read it. I could hardly believe my eyes when, a few days later, with the aid of my new magnifying machine, I read what came close to being a "rave" review, in which she said it was "one of those can't put it down" books. That got the ball rolling.

We also had a small daily paper that published nothing but local news. I believe it was called, "The Mailbox." It was one of those free papers that could be picked up at checkout counters, but it had a good circulation. I called its editor, who was a good friend of mine, and he sent out his lone reporter (who did double duty as a cameraman) for an interview. The very next day, I was featured in a half-page story, replete with pictures, as "Valdosta's newest and oldest author, legally blind Jim Hammond, who at age 83, had published his very first book." A couple of days later, *The Valdosta Daily Times* sent out a reporter who spent a full half day interviewing me. He wrote a wonderful and highly flattering story with a picture of me surrounded by my large-screen computer, my big magnifying machine and my printer, while sitting at my keyboard typing.

The stories in both papers focused on the uniqueness of the fact that an 83-year-old blind man could write a book with no help. I knew it was this that engendered all the interest—not the quality of my book, but I didn't care. I knew it would help my book sell. And I loved all that publicity and I loved it even more because it was free.

1997

I gave a copy of my book to the manager of our largest bookstore, Books-A-Million, and one to the owner of our largest gift shop that also had a book department. Both had read the newspaper stories and each asked me to do a book signing and one was scheduled then and there.

Both papers very generously ran notices giving date and time of each signing but I was still concerned that only a few would come. To avoid the embarrassing possibility that no one would show up, I mailed 140 invitations to my good Valdosta friends, the majority of whom were my fellow Rotary Club members, pleading with them to come. A copy of that invitation is included on the next page.

The first signing was at the gift shop and I was not prepared for the turnout. My wonderful friends flocked in by the dozens. Soon after the doors opened, a line began to form and there were very few times throughout the day when there was no line at all. Mildly stated, I was absolutely flabbergasted.

I soon regained my composure and began having the time of my life. Most of my friends knew each other and it was like an all-day party with an ever-changing group of guests. Everybody had fun visiting with so many friends, but I had the most fun of all. I had a great time teasing my friends. After greeting them as they came in, I assumed a mightier-than-thou attitude as if I were a real celebrity, and in a haughty voice and a dramatic sweep of my arm, I'd direct them to take their place at the end of the line.

A reporter from each newspaper covered my event, took pictures, and included one in nice follow-up stories. More great, free advertising!

Continued on page 94

What a Beautiful Sunset

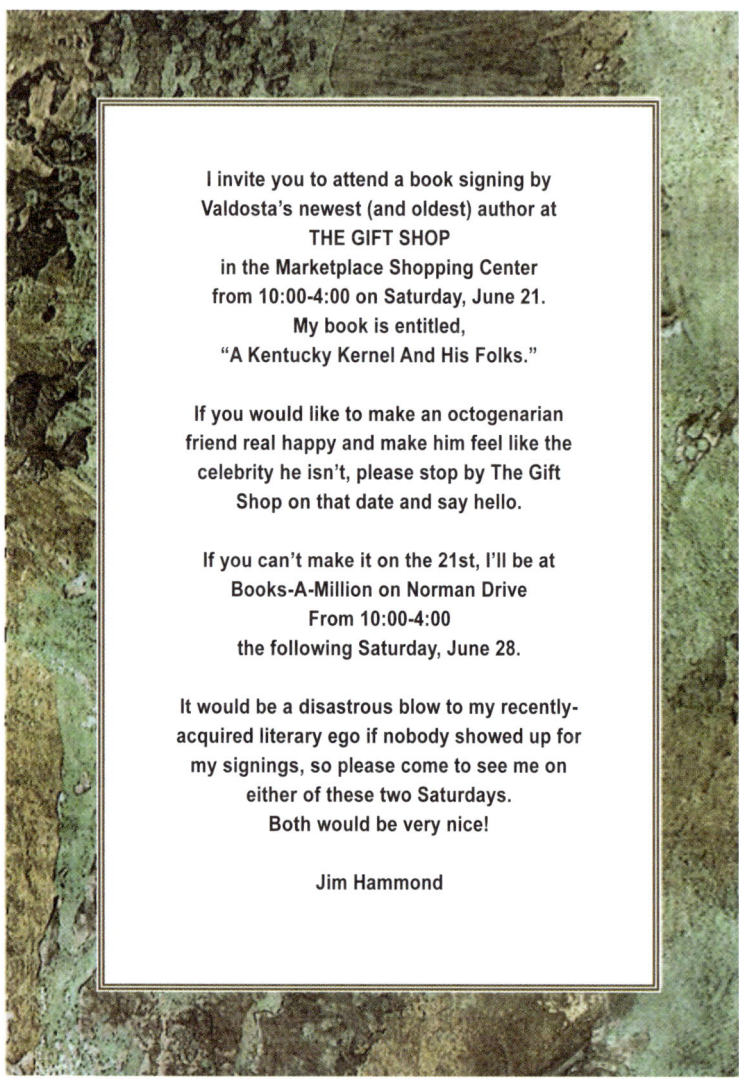

I invite you to attend a book signing by
Valdosta's newest (and oldest) author at
THE GIFT SHOP
in the Marketplace Shopping Center
from 10:00-4:00 on Saturday, June 21.
My book is entitled,
"A Kentucky Kernel And His Folks."

If you would like to make an octogenarian friend real happy and make him feel like the celebrity he isn't, please stop by The Gift Shop on that date and say hello.

If you can't make it on the 21st, I'll be at
Books-A-Million on Norman Drive
From 10:00-4:00
the following Saturday, June 28.

It would be a disastrous blow to my recently-acquired literary ego if nobody showed up for my signings, so please come to see me on either of these two Saturdays.
Both would be very nice!

Jim Hammond

I autographed books in Valdosta at The Gift Shop on June 21, 1997 and at Books-A-Million on June 28, 1997. Here I am at The Gift Shop autographing a book for Frances Kafoures while Carey looks on.

Here I am at Books-A-Million autographing a book for good friend and former neighbor, Ann Smith, standing on the left, while another customer waits her turn. I autographed 158 copies during these two signings.

James Hammond Still Sees Life Clearly Despite Failing Eyesight

James H. Hammond, an 83-year-old, legally blind Valdostan, is shown with computer equipment that allowed him to write his first book.

By Charles Shiver
Mailbox Post Staff Writer

An eye disease has stolen most of 83-year-old Valdostan James H. Hammond's vision. But with his mind's eye still seeing most of the 20th Century, he has published his first book, an autobiography called "A Kentucky Kernel & His Folks."

Hammond, a retired businessman, will be at a book-signing 10 a.m.-4 p.m. Saturday at Books A Million.

"I've enjoyed writing this book more than anything else I've ever done," Hammond said. "It was wonderful for me because it made my transition from being a seeing person to a legally blind person really easy. It couldn't have come at a better time."

Macular degeneration, an age-related disease affecting Hammond's central vision, has taken away his ability to read printed material and drive a car.

But his brother-in-law, Charlie Aldridge, set up a closed-circuit television system in Hammond's bedroom that expands the size of text on a screen so Hammond can see to read and write. Also, another computer has enlarged text on its screen and reads back to Hammond what he has written. The system "almost makes it fun to be visually impaired," he said.

Thus empowered, Hammond spent 10 months (December 1995-October 1996) on a keyboard as he wrote the story of his life and family and friends that have passed through it.

Born on a Logan County, Ky., farm in April 1914, Hammond had a 25-year career in sales management with Allstate Insurance Co. Enjoying travel, he has lived in 10 different states and 14 different cities. The only condition required by his wife Carey for following him around was they could only live south of the Mason-Dixon line.

Hammond said his book reflects "a remarkably happy life - free of the problems most people have faced."

Still, he has met his fair share of interesting characters. One of them was a recluse who lived in a backwoods shack filled with books near Hammond's boyhood home. The hermit, a former Rhodes Scholar at Oxford University, had retreated into seclusion after his fiancee drowned. Although Hammond and other children were afraid of the man, Hammond's father became good friends with the hermit by talking with him about their common love - books.

About 20 years ago, Hammond began breeding exotic birds as a hobby.

He retired from Allstate in 1974 and moved to Valdosta in 1979, when he had time to convert his love of animals into a second career.

In 1980, he opened Wings Pet Shop in the old Brookwood Plaza Shopping Center and began selling everything from pot-bellied pigs and pygmy goats to hundreds of white mice and large, white rats, used as snake food.

His favorite bird was Festus, a talking blue and gold macaw whose favorite trick was hanging upside down by one toenail from the store's ceiling and screaming for help. Hammond was forced to come to his store at 11 one night after a lady called and insisted he "rescue" Festus.

Festus died after getting a shock from chewing wires inside a light fixture.

Festus was so popular that Hammond had to display a poster explaining the death in detail to the many customers who asked about the bird.

On Jan. 1, 1993, Hammond's deteriorating vision forced him to sell Wings.

However, the sale didn't include his bird farm and bird breeding business.

"I stay active even though my eyesight is so bad that I can't drive anymore," he said. "My wife has been good about being my chauffeur." He attends the Valdosta Rotary Club each Wednesday and church each Sunday. In addition, he gardens, growing a colorful melange of flowers around his home, and works out six days a week at the YMCA.

Hammond said his next book could be about his wife's first cousin, an intriguing lady. She jilted a boyfriend who longed for her the rest of his life and left her $3 million in his will, Hammond said.

Continued on next page

What a Beautiful Sunset

Continued from previous page

Hammond is grateful to his son, Mac, a minister, and daughter-in-law, Lynne, for using the resources of their church, Living Word Christian Center, in printing "A Kentucky Kernel."

The Minneapolis, Minn.-based ministry has more than 5,000 members and is conducting a fund-raising campaign for a $20 million religious complex to include a K-12 school and 15,000-seat sanctuary.

Mac Hammond conducts a national TV service every Sunday morning on Trinity Broadcasting Network, which reaches 45 million homes.

"It is absolutely incomprehensible to Carey and me that we produced a son with Mac's brain power and ability," Hammond writes in his book. "To say we are proud of him and Lynne would be the understatement of the year."

Those wishing to get a copy of "A Kentucky Kernel," may go to Books A Million or The Gift Shop, or call Hammond at his home at 244-8084.

Continued from page 89

Although quite successful by the store's standards, my second signing a week later at Books-A-Million was somewhat of an anticlimax for me. Lines formed only two or three times during the whole day but the long one occurred at the very most auspicious moment.

It was about noon when two of my most favorite people, my niece, Nancy Boyd Hammond Hughes (now deceased), and her daughter, my great niece, Amy Hughes Wood, from Bowling Green, Kentucky, slipped in at the end of the line without my knowing it.

I had no reason to think they were anywhere but at home 450 to 500 miles away. They wanted to surprise me and did they ever! Due to my poor vision, I did not see them until I had autographed a book for a lady in front of Nancy Boyd. I then looked up into the smiling, beautiful, big, dark-brown eyes of my beloved niece. I startled everyone in that big store when I shrieked, NANCY BOYD! It was one of the most humbling experiences of my life to know that those

1997

two wonderful human beings loved me enough to get up in the wee hours of the morning and drive nonstop for nine or ten hours to Books-A-Million in Valdosta, Georgia, for my book signing. I was even more touched when I learned it had to be an almost turn-around trip. Nancy Boyd was a schoolteacher and had to be back in her classroom at eight o'clock Monday morning. Almost back-to-back nine to 10 hour drives, few people in this world would have done such a thing for an uncle. What a beautiful expression of their love for me by those two dearly loved ones! There's no better feeling than to know you are loved by someone you love.

I wrote this book primarily for the benefit of my immediate family, other relatives, and a few good friends who might be interested. After I finished it and before I sent it to the printers, I sent a manuscript to three relatives and three friends and asked for their critical opinion. I made a point of sending it to only those I could trust to give me their honest opinion without fear of being critical. When I received six very enthusiastic reviews with no real criticism from anybody, I decided to have 1,500 copies printed and try to sell them through the local bookstores in Valdosta and the one bookstore in my hometown, Franklin, Kentucky.

They went on sale in the Valdosta bookstores on June 28, 1997. Although sales slowed down after about six months, at the end of one year all had been sold. Of course, I'll never know, but I do believe I could have sold a lot more books and maybe hit it big time had it been properly promoted. But at age 83, I had neither the time, energy, nor the inclination to do so. After all, it brought me enough pleasure, fun, and excitement during that year to

Continued on page 97

What a Beautiful Sunset

Valdostan's autobiography full

Author James Herschel Hammond lives and worked right here in Valdosta. I have known him for many years; in fact, one of my daughters worked for him in his Wings Pet Shop. He and I also attend the same church, Christ Episcopal.

Several weeks ago he came into the office and asked me to read and tell him what I thought of his book that he had written, *A Kentucky Kernel and his folks.*

BOOKWORM

EDITH SMITH

It is the story of his life. It marks the end of the growing up years for him and the beginning of his marriage. It also tells of being a father and of his career that took him to many cities and many challenging assignments before he finally came to Valdosta to settle down.

He was born on a farm in Logan County, Ky., on April 5, 1914.

This was the same year that World War I started.

Jim Hammond was number six of seven children born to Herschel Lyon" and Estelle Bradshaw Hammond.

His father grew up in Franklin, Ky., graduated from high school and from Southern Medical School of Osteopathy. His father and mother married in 1899 and moved to nearby Tennessee where he set up a practice. After two years, he gave up his full-time practice and moved to a farm in Logan County where he became a full-time farmer and a part-time doctor.

It was here that Jim was born.

Throughout the book you will see where Jim has written about his family. They were very close, and he remembers only good things about his childhood.

His daddy was kind and fair, but when he spoke, Jim knew not to argue but to immediately obey. His father teased and loved his mother very much, and it spilled over to Jim.

Growing up in a household with six other children, you learn to give and take.

On March 30, 1930, one week after Jim's 16th birthday, he awoke to a beautiful, sunny spring day. His mother was healthy and went about her duties, one of which was cleaning some dirt that his father had spilled on the floor fixing a window box. Jim and his sister, Jeanette, got home from school, and Jim had gone into the walk-in pantry to get a piece of cake. He heard his mother fall, and he rushed to her. "Hurry, get your daddy," she said.

1997

The Valdosta Daily Times

# of love, happiness, contentment

She never regained consciousness; a cerebral hemorrhage claimed her life.

Jim was determined to finish school and to do better and win all of the school awards. He graduated in 1932 and was chosen as valedictorian.

He joined the U.S. Navy in October 1932.

On July 6, 1934, he was sworn in as a midshipman at the U.S. Naval Academy at Annapolis.

Although he studied very hard and did well in all other subjects, he did not have the qualifications for higher math. He did not quite make the grade on calculus and, along with about 100 others, was discharged on June 30, 1935.

After his discharge he got a job in New York. He bought a 3-cent newspaper that changed his life forever.

He got a job working for New York Terminal Warehouse Company based in Atlanta.

Jim found a place with room and board at #1 Peachtree Circle, Pattillo Villa. It was here that he met his beloved Carey.

She was Carey Willis and had the best figure in the house. They began dating but had a disagreement that lasted a year and three months. They did get back together and married finally.

Carey was a wonderful wife and mother. Jim traveled extensively in his job, and Carey was ready to move at a moment's notice.

Their lives are full of adventure, places, people and things.

This book is full of love, happiness and contentment. In today's world, this is hard to believe.

You won't want to miss getting this book and having it signed by the 83-year-old author who still has lots of life left to live. He will be signing copies today at the Gi Shop and on June 28 at Books-a-Million.

Continued from page 95

last me a lifetime. Such a rewarding experience comes to very few people after the age of 80 and I consider myself blessed beyond measure.

The fun and excitement didn't end with my book signings but continued full blast throughout the year. I was in constant demand as a speaker at book clubs, my Rotary Club, other civic clubs, several church groups, schools, and various other groups.

What a Beautiful Sunset

I spent endless hours at my computer writing thank you notes for countless phone calls and letters about my book. I still have a big thick file that I pretentiously labeled my "Fan Club File." Some day when I have time, it will be fun to sit down and read some of them again.

Carey always sat at the speaker's table with me when I spoke to the various groups and I loved introducing her. My favorite introduction was when I spoke to my Rotary Club. It went like this. "Way back yonder in 1939, I married a beautiful girl from Columbus, Georgia, named Mary Carey Willis. Now, 58 years later, she's still lovely to look at, delightful to know, and heaven to kiss. Here she is, my fellow Rotarians. You be the judge." Their enthusiastic applause was tempered only by their obvious regret over having to take my word for the "heaven to kiss" part. I was delighted for all to see that my beautiful bride of 58 years could still blush as charmingly as a shy, 16-year-old high school girl.

Throughout the year, my book doings were interspersed with more other activities than now seems possible. Here are some of them:

In July, we took a 10-day vacation with all the family at Pelican Lake in northern Minnesota. Next came the sale, in August, of the beautiful house we built three years earlier as our perfect and final retirement home. At this point, I'd like to quote the last paragraph of my book, *A Kentucky Kernel & His Folks*.

"Now that I have told my story and completed another challenging project, this aging Kentucky farm boy can see a worried, apprehensive look in Carey's eyes. It seemed to say, 'What's next? Not another move!' I hope she will be saved by my computer. I plan to use it to explore the fascinating world of the Internet, an exciting adventure that should keep me happily occupied well into the 21st century."

That worried look in Carey's eyes turned out to be nothing short of prophetic. I thought my penchant for moving would die with my old age, but it didn't. I didn't know that it was just lying there dormant for a short season.

A 10-foot backyard, wood-panel fence separated our property from that of Langdale Place, a classy retirement complex. We had several friends who had sold their homes and moved there. Without exception, they loved it. When I noticed that a new annex to the main building at Langdale Place was under construction, I felt my "penchant for moving" begin to stir. When they told me in March it would be ready for occupancy in August, I selected the choice, first-floor apartment and made a deposit with a 30-day notice deposit refund agreement. That gave me five months to do a hard-sell job on Carey. The idea of a totally new and very different lifestyle was very exciting to me.

As the first step in my well-planned sales strategy, I took one of our friends who lived there into my confidence. I told him I'd love to live there and I knew Carey would too, but we'd have to do a real sales job on her as she dearly loved our new home where we'd lived only three years. As I had hoped he'd do, he invited us to dinner, promised to give us a guided tour of the facility, tell Carey all about the many wonderful amenities, and not reveal our motive. It worked like a charm. The food was fabulous (a huge plus for Carey), she loved the décor and the elegant furnishings of all the common areas, which included bridge rooms, a library, TV rooms, lounges, and a huge room for large receptions and large parties. It was called the Rose Room and it was impressive. I could tell

What a Beautiful Sunset

by Carey's reaction that my sales job was a piece of cake. I mentally canceled steps 2, 3 and 4 of my sales plan.

Before we could put our house on the market, the word that we were selling spread through our neighborhood. A new doctor in town stopped by, asked if we'd show it and we did. After a brief walk-through, he asked me how much, I gave him a quite inflated price without batting an eye, he asked if that was my bottom price, I said yes, he asked how much the deposit was, I told him and he wrote a check. It was actually that simple. On top of that, he agreed to let us stay in the house until our apartment was ready. My guardian angel, who is always hovering around, must have worked very hard that day.

On August 27, 1997, we said goodbye to the last house we ever lived in. Carey was in tears as she loved that house. The move was made easy by the help we received from Mac, Lynne, grandson John, and his wife, Beckey, who had flown down from Minneapolis for that purpose. We moved into our new apartment home at Langdale Place in Valdosta, Georgia. Downsizing was our only problem. Carey wanted to part with none of her treasures and there was room for less than half of them in our two-bedroom apartment. It was a very traumatic experience for her. It made it a little easier for her to know that it would be divided between our three grandchildren. John rented a moving van and drove it back to Minneapolis loaded with our stuff and put it in a storage warehouse until it could be divided.

To add drama and excitement to our moving adventure, Carey plunged head first into a clothes closet and broke her right arm just below her shoulder on the very day our furniture was moved into our apartment. She was rushed to the hospital for emergency surgery. Great planning! She didn't have to unpack one thing. Fortunately, two of our family muscle men, Mac and John, were there to do all the heavy lifting. When Carey came home from the hospital five days later, everything was unpacked and in place. Carey was disabled for two weeks and I had to do everything, even bathe her, which was fun as I found things I'd forgotten she had. She let her ordeal slow her down very little.

We loved living at Langdale Place. We didn't anticipate how nice it would be not to have the worry of planning, shopping for, and cooking our meals, to say nothing of maid and laundry service, or the availability of courtesy transportation for me whenever I needed it. Carey still drove and chauffeured me when she could. The food was fabulous and I had to workout twice as hard at the "Y" in order not to gain weight. All in all, it was a pleasant place to live.

On November 3, 1997, our beautiful baby granddaughter, LucyHart, gave birth to our third great grandson, Micheal Lane (Lane) Minton, Jr. Could our little LucyHart have been old enough to birth a bouncing baby boy? I suppose so as she was 24, but how did the years pass so quickly?

Next came a Caribbean cruise on November 15 with our long-time friends from Virginia, Alice and Johnny Goodwin. Then followed a trip to Minneapolis for Thanksgiving with our family. We closed out 1997 spending the Christmas holidays at a fabulous hotel on Marco Island (off the southwest tip of Florida) with our family (14 of us).

What a year! Sounds exhausting, doesn't it? Especially for a couple in their 80s, and maybe it was. But nine years later, I remember it as among the busiest, happiest, most exciting, and most rewarding years of my life.

What a Beautiful Sunset

We vacationed with Mac and family in July 1997 at their lake house in northern Minnesota. Carey and I are getting out of Mac's boat.

On November 15, 1997, we went on another Caribbean cruise with our long-time friends from Richmond, Virginia, Alice and Johnny. Alice and Johnny are pictured here.

Chapter 5

1998

This may sound repetitious and it is but it is factual, as 1998 really was another fast-moving and eventful year for us. It included four trips to Minneapolis (Easter, July 4th, Labor Day and Thanksgiving), one to Kentucky, and one to Ponte Vedra, FL. It was great that all our grandchildren and our great grandchildren, as well as Mac and Lynne, lived in Minneapolis and we could visit with all of them on each trip.

Our trip to Franklin, Kentucky was for my 66th high school class reunion. Although I graduated in 1932, the reunion was for everyone still living who graduated in or before 1940. So there was quite a bunch of us, 113 to be exact. I was asked to be the speaker with my book as my subject. I got a wonderful response as I remembered a lot of funny stories about the folks I grew up with. After my speech, most of them stood in line for an autographed copy of my book and I sold a bunch of them.

The next day, I held a very successful book signing at Bridgette's Books, Franklin's only bookstore. In addition to selling lots of books, it was great talking to so many people I had not seen in 66 years. Everyone's warm and enthusiastic welcome home made me feel great.

What a Beautiful Sunset

We vacationed over the Memorial Day weekend with our long-time friends from Atlanta, Earl and Betty Barton (both are now deceased), on a six-day stay at a swanky and very expensive resort, the Ponte Vedra Inn and Club. To a child of the Great Depression, it seemed a lot to pay for such a short stay even though we had a wonderful time. But the Bartons would be fun to vacation with anywhere.

When we went to Ponte Vedra, the Bartons drove down from Atlanta and stopped in Valdosta so we could ride with them. They left Atlanta quite early and asked us to meet them at the Cracker Barrel for breakfast. A week or so earlier, Earl slipped on a wet bathroom floor at the "Y," fell backwards and put both hands behind him to break the fall. Instead of breaking the fall, he broke both arms just above each wrist. Each arm was put into a cast from shoulder to fingertips. Of course, Betty had to drive. We arrived at the Cracker Barrel before they did and were sitting in rocking chairs on the front porch when Betty wheeled into the parking lot, parked the car, opened the door, got out, slammed the door shut real hard, and walked across the parking lot toward us.

In the meantime, Earl slipped under the wheel with the two casts sticking straight out and he re-parked that car with considerable difficulty. I said, "Betty, what in the world is going on?" She said she told him, "If you don't like the way I parked it, park the damn thing yourself." Poor Earl! Betty's reaction to Earl's thoughtful parking tips reminded me of the time Carey actually almost dumped me out on the side of the road for merely making a few helpful driving suggestions.

1998

I decided then and there that Carey and Betty were typical of ALL women drivers—very touchy about their lack of driving skills and much too easily moved to anger by the patient and well-intended constructive criticism by their husbands. Women drivers! Please excuse my bold outburst. Of course, if Carey were here to read it, I wouldn't have the courage to write it. Do I hear a rumbling noise coming down from up above? If so, heaven help me please!

Carey's memory problem and her high-blood pressure had no effect whatever on her activities or her happy attitude toward life and my book continued to keep me busy.

Carey on our porch at Langdale Place in the early spring of 1998.

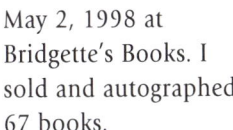

May 2, 1998 at Bridgette's Books. I sold and autographed 67 books.

What a Beautiful Sunset

May 22 to May 26, 1998. On a four-day vacation over the Memorial Day weekend at the Ponte Vedra Club and Inn at Ponte Vedra, Florida with our long-time friends from Atlanta, Betty and Earl Barton.

1998

THE BIG PICTURE

Contributed photo

VISION QUEST: Jim Hammond, Valdosta, says these specially equipped monitors aid his sight.

Man keeps a hold on his world with a little help from some big screens

By Dean Poling
dean.poling@thomnews.com

VALDOSTA — Letters as large as the words on a billboard cramp the space on Jim Hammond's computer screen.

Yet, they are just big enough for Hammond to see. Just big enough for Hammond to maintain the life he has always loved.

Shortly after Hammond turned 80, he was diagnosed with an age-related eye disease known as macular degeneration — a condition which erodes the central vision while leaving the peripheral vision untouched.

Hammond explains that he can look a person in the eye and that person's face is a blur of features, but everything around that person — the areas where Hammond's eyes aren't focused, such as a person's hands holding and writing in a note pad — are as clear as anything you might catch out of the corner of your eye.

"I couldn't see to sign a

Continued on next page

107

What a Beautiful Sunset

Continued from previous page

check even. I had handled our finances for years," Hammond says, referring to his wife, Carey. "I just couldn't handle much of the paperwork that I normally did and enjoyed doing."

It took some money and a little thought, but Hammond was able to reclaim this part of his life. He purchased a large-screen computer, which he can manipulate the size of text until he can see it. While suffering macular degeneration, Hammond was able to write a book on his life "A Kentucky Kernel."

A magnified life

Hammond also purchased a Magnum Magnifier, which works like an overhead projector. Now 86, Hammond places bills and his checkbook on the platform under the Magnifier's screen. By adjusting the size of the image, he is able to read the bills or balance the checkbook on the screen. He can even write and sign the checks using this same method. "My handwriting's a bit shaky, but it works," Hammond says.

The Magnum Magnifier can allow him to read newspapers and books, but he doesn't use it for these purposes, saying his wife reads him the paper and he usually enjoys audio books. He doesn't read from the Magnifier because the type is so large that it requires constant movement across the screen to follow a line which leaves him dizzy.

And when Hammond hugs his little great-grandchildren, he can't see the features of their faces, but he knows what they look like. By placing the youngsters' photographs into the Magnifier, he can see their faces.

The cost

The computer and Magnifier set-up cost Hammond about $15,000.

But that was a few years ago.

Computer hardware and software are less expensive today, and there are less expensive brands available as well.

"The 80s have been one of the busiest times of my life," says Hammond, who walks daily and is preparing for the state's Golden Olympics competition.

"This gave me my life back, and I just wanted to let others know that this is available. I just wish that there was some way to have one of the screens everywhere for everything."

Chapter 6

1999

Years ago, I never dreamed we'd be around at the end of this century and the beginning of the new millennium but I sure was glad we were. Here in brief was our year in 1999. Spent three days at St. Petersburg Beach in March for a great family reunion (Carey's side). We celebrated my 85th birthday on April 5. I Loved all my cards, but especially the one from Dave Shelley that read, "Old folks must be careful not to break things—like wind." Went on a fun 10-day western Caribbean cruise in April with old friends, two couples from Charleston, SC, with stops in Mexico, Central America, Panama Canal, and Columbia, South America.

We took a fabulous trip to Cambridge, Mass., to attend reception and dinner honoring my nephew, Jerry Murphy, who was Dean of the Harvard Graduate School of Education. A 3.4 million-dollar chair was endowed in his honor—a very impressive affair. It was almost like a family reunion as a large number of my relatives were among the 400 guests. We spent four one-week visits with Mac and family (in Valdosta in April and September and in Minneapolis in July and Thanksgiving). On November 14, 1999, our second great granddaughter, Caroline Minton, was born. When we were in Minneapolis for Thanksgiving, it was immediately obvious that little Caroline would be just as beautiful as her mother, LucyHart. We saw her again when we spent the Christmas and New Year holidays in Minneapolis with the family. While there, Mac and Lynne had a big, fabulous celebration party for our 60th wedding anniversary on December 31, the last day of the 20th century.

Health wise, we were fine. I was still keeping physically fit by working out almost daily at the "Y," where I reaped another benefit—great fellowship with several good friends who also worked out there. At that time, Carey had very few aches and pains except for an arthritic knee. She still played lots of duplicate bridge and won frequently. Overall, we were in fine shape.

We still enjoyed life at Langdale Place. My only reservation about moving there was that I might not like living in such close proximity to so many old folks, but we liked and enjoyed almost everyone. We had complete privacy in our apartment as no one dropped in uninvited. Yet there was much visiting in the common areas. It was nice that we could socialize as much or as little as we chose. Despite the advanced age and diminished physical activities of many of our fellow residents, many were clever, witty, and interesting folks who were fun to be with.

Carey and I on her 84th birthday (February 6, 1999) with flowers Mac and Lynne sent her.

1999

Carey with the flowers they sent her on Mother's Day 1999.

REGAL PRINCESS   PANAMA CANAL   PRINCESS CRUISES

April 7-17, 1999, aboard the Regal Princess (Love Boat) on a cruise to the Grand Cayman Islands, Mexico (Cozumel), Central America (Panama Canal), Costa Rica (Limon) and South America

Continued on next page

What a Beautiful Sunset

Continued from previous page

(Cartagena, Columbia) with two couples Gene & Grace Quillian and Bill & Nelie Thomas from Charleston, SC. We have been friends since we lived in Charleston for two years right after the war (1945-47). Charlie and Sybil Mashburn also had reservations for the trip but had to cancel at the last minute due to an emergency medical problem. This was a great disappointment to all of us as this same group had enjoyed a wonderful Caribbean cruise together two years earlier. Florrie and Clarence Irwin, good friends of the Mashburns, went along instead. All of us are pictured below at the dinner table. Standing are Florrie and Clarence Irwin. Seated from left to right are Gene & Grace Quillian, Carey & I, and Bill & Nelie Thomas.

On December 31, 1999, Mac and Lynne hosted at their home in Minneapolis, a beautiful 60th wedding anniversary celebration for us, which was attended by many friends and relatives. They presented us with two beautifully bound and illustrated memory books with artfully arranged greetings, letters, photos, and funny stories from old friends and relatives from across the country. From left to right: Mac, me, Carey and Lynne looking through the memory book.

1999

Edward and Jane Willis (Carey's brother and sister-in-law) me, Carey, and Mac

More anniversary photos. LucyHart, Lynne, Beckey, and Kristin.

What a Beautiful Sunset

Kristen, Carey, and I.

Carey became a member of the Wednesday Bridge Club shortly after we moved to Valdosta in 1979 and her membership terminated 22 years later when we moved to Minneapolis in 2001. This picture was taken May 1, 1999. They are, from left to right, Liavan Sims, Betty Tillman, Carey, Marion Myddleton, Helen Smith, Doris Budd, Barbara Norris, and Vela Dean.

Chapter 7

2000

Other than five great one-week visits with Mac and family (three in Minneapolis and two at the beach in Destin, FL), we took only one trip, far less than any year since my retirement from Allstate Insurance Company on January 1, 1974, more than 32 years ago.

In May, we joined 52 other Valdosta seniors, most of whom we already knew, on a bus tour of the Upper Peninsular of Michigan, the main attraction being the Tulip Festival in Holland, MI. Amazingly, that 2,500-mile bus ride wasn't in the least exhausting as the seats were very comfortable and we made frequent rest stops. It was very enjoyable from start to finish, thanks to beautiful scenery, a most interesting area of our country that was new to us, and great fellowship with a bus load of friendly and interesting fellow travelers.

Now for my only noteworthy accomplishment in the year 2000—I won a gold medal in a track event, the 100-meter run in the Georgia Golden Olympics. How could that possibly be when never in my life had I participated in any competitive sport, other than golf—and I was not very good at that? It's not a short story but I'll tell it anyway.

What a Beautiful Sunset

What prompted me to participate in the Georgia Golden Olympics? A friend with whom I worked out at the "Y," knowing I was quite physically fit for my age, told me about the Georgia Golden Olympics, as well as the National Senior Olympics (a part of the same organization). It's amazing that I had never heard of either as up to 800 senior athletes participate annually in Georgia in 18 different sports, and up to 12,000 in the nationals. The nationals are held biannually on the odd years and the state games on the even years. To qualify for the nationals, one must win first, second, or third place in the preceding year's state games. The idea immediately appealed to me. It sounded like an exciting adventure.

Why track? I went to a country school back in the dark ages when I'd never heard of such a thing as a track team. Nevertheless, a bunch of us barefoot country boys would often get together and race each other. I loved it as I always won, even against the older boys. When deciding on a sport to compete in, I thought back to those barefoot races and remembered how great it felt to always win. I knew it had to be track.

The Georgia Golden Olympic games were held at Warner Robins Air Force Base (near Macon) on September 21-23, 2000. I entered that race without ever having run on a track and I won a gold medal. I won it with such an extremely slow running time that I'm now ashamed for anyone to know that it took me 30 seconds to run 100 meters. It just so happened that the runners in my age group that particular year would have had trouble outrunning someone in a wheelchair. But that didn't matter to me at the moment. As state champion, I was qualified to compete in the National Senior Olympics in Baton Rouge, Louisiana in July 2001. This part of my story will be continued in upcoming Chapter 8 which covers our activities during the year of 2001.

I will close this chapter on a sad note to an otherwise happy year—the death of a dear and beloved friend, Alice Goodwin of Richmond, Virginia. Alice and John had been our best friends for 63 years when she died. We had taken many wonderful trips together over the years. Our first vacation together was at St. Simons Island, Georgia in 1940 when both of us were newlyweds. Our last visit was on a Caribbean Cruise in 1998. At our age, we should have been prepared for the loss of such a good friend but we were not. It was very hard for us then and it is still hard for me to accept the reality of her death.

We celebrated our 61st wedding anniversary on December 31, 2000. The Lord had to have our old age in mind when He brought us together so long ago. In our old age, she was my eyes and I was her memory.

In October 1999, it was necessary for us to have our 13-year-old white poodle, Daisy, put to sleep due to a malignant tumor. When we were visiting Mac during Thanksgiving 1999, he bought a 1½ pound nine-week-old Yorkshire Terrier puppy and gave it to us. We named him Rambeau. He is now full grown and weighs only 3½ pounds. This is Daisy shortly before her death.

This is Rambeau on his first birthday on October 1, 2000.

Georgia Golden Olympics 2000

TODAY'S VALDOSTA COMMUNITY CHAMPION

Jim Hammond, 86, is a legally blind Valdosta man who took a gold medal in a track event over the weekend at Warner Robins.

HAMMOND

JIM HAMMOND: Gold medal winner

James H. Hammond, known by most folks as Jim, is an 86-year-old Valdosta resident who is legally blind. His handicap has not held him back from enjoying local activities. Over the weekend, he won the gold medal in a track event, the 100-meter run, at the Georgia Golden Olympic games held at Robins Air Force Base, Warner Robins. Hammond and his wife of 60 years, Carey, live at Langdale Place. He is a senior-active member of the Valdosta Rotary Club, a charter member of the Valdosta chapter of Sons of the American Revolution and is an active member of Christ Episcopal Church.

Chapter 8

2001

On November 24, 2001, Carey and I did what seemed to many a shocking thing for a couple in their 80s to do—we moved AGAIN! For us "to move again" should have been no shock to anyone, as at that point, we had done it more than 20 times, but the "from where to where" was a shock to all. This time for the first time, we aimed NORTH, took a giant leap from south Georgia and landed in the middle of the land of 10,000 frozen lakes—Minnesota.

When Mac first suggested our moving to Minneapolis to be close to our whole family, we shrugged it off as being out of the question. Shortly after they moved to Minnesota in 1978, we visited them in the dead of winter and the temperature never once rose above eight degrees below zero during all of that seven-day, first visit. After that we strictly limited our visits to the spring, summer, fall, and early winter (Thanksgiving and Christmas) months for obvious reasons.

When Mac planted that seed in the fertile soil of my "penchant for moving," it quickly sprouted, took root, grew, and flourished (as Mac knew it would); the end result being, our move out of that delightfully warm south Georgia

What a Beautiful Sunset

sunshine into the middle of a massive Minnesota, wind-driven snowstorm on November 24, 2001.

How could this be in view of my long-ago promise to Carey that I'd never ask her to move north of the Mason-Dixon line. For a couple in their 80s to be moving to the frigid north when most rational senior citizens in the far north were moving south defied all logic when both Carey and I loved Valdosta, the warm weather, our many, many great Valdosta friends and everything about our lives there. I thought my wanderlust gene had been put to sleep for the duration of my old age, but not so. Mac's mention of the word "moving" awoke my sleeping tiger and it was on the prowl again. The inbred nature of the beast to keep on moving on was too strong for me to control, not that I tried very hard.

So we moved again. This time into a nice, spacious apartment in a beautiful retirement complex called Rose Arbor in Maple Grove, MN (a Minneapolis suburb). Rose Arbor was located within an eight-mile radius of Mac and Lynne, our three grandchildren and our six great grandchildren. Once again, my moving gene continued its unbroken record of never having let me down. In very short order, both Carey and I knew beyond a shadow of a doubt that our decision to move was a great one. In one's old age, there's no greater joy than to be completely surrounded by a large, loving family like ours.

The third major event in 2001 was especially thrilling to me. It's a quite long story about the birth and growth of my career as a senior athlete in the field of track. Its birth and early beginning were covered in the preceding chapter and left off with my winning a gold medal in the 100-meter

2001

track event in the September 2000 Georgia Golden Olympic Games. The story picks up there and continues herewith.

In September 2000, I won the gold medal in the 100-meter race in the Georgia Golden Olympics with an embarrassingly slow running time of 30 seconds, but at least it did qualify me for participation in the National Senior Olympic Games in Baton Rouge, Louisiana in July 2001.

When I returned to Valdosta after winning the gold medal, I continued my workouts at the "Y" five days every week. In addition, each day before going to the "Y," I practiced running 100 meters as fast as I could, over and over again for about 20 to 30 minutes at a nearby high-school track. After sticking to this routine religiously for six months, I had reduced my running time from 30 seconds to 23 seconds, but no matter how hard I tried, using every ounce of my energy, I could reduce my running time no farther.

Around the first of April 2001, three months before the National Senior Olympic games would be held in Baton Rouge, I called Vicki Pilgrim, State Coordinator for the Georgia Golden Olympics in Atlanta and asked her if she could give me an idea of what it would take to win the 100-meter race in the nationals. When she told me from 18 to 18.5 seconds, I was ready to throw in the towel. However, before I hung up the phone, she made me promise that I'd find a good track coach and go for the gold. My guardian angel must have listened in on that phone conversation. The very next day, a friend gave me the phone number of a young teacher at Hahira High School who also coached track. His name was Bruce Beal and he was a former LSU track star and a Southeastern Conference titleholder in the 100-meter run. I called him and he agreed to meet me at the

"Y" that evening to talk about it. He said he'd coach me only if I could convince him I was really serious about winning. To make a long story a little shorter, I convinced him I was serious, he agreed to coach me and make me a winner and that is exactly what he did.

I was astounded by his dedication and determination to make me a winner. He was a slave driver who showed me no mercy and no respect for my age when it came to hard work. A number of times, I was tempted to quit but my pride and my respect for my coach wouldn't let me do it.

When he spent more time with me than he had agreed to, he would not accept extra pay, saying my winning would be payment enough. On three different occasions, he took time away from his young family and drove me to the Florida State University track in Tallahassee where open track meets were held every Monday night. He wanted me to get experience running in real track meets. He refused to accept any compensation for the time involved on these trips (about four hours) and it was with reluctance that he allowed me to fill his tank with gas.

On our last trip to Tallahassee before I left for Baton Rouge, I ran it in 18.5 seconds, my best time ever. While talking to another coach there, I overheard him say, "Now I know I've got a winner." By this time, he was not only my coach, he was my friend. With such dedication to my cause, I had no choice. I had to win at least a bronze. His last words of advice were, "Shut out everything that's going on around you and focus on nothing but crossing the finish line first," advice I wish I had remembered in my first national race.

Mac flew down from Minneapolis to Valdosta, picked up Carey and me and flew us to Baton Rouge the day before my race. He brought our grandson Jim, his wife Kristin and their two children, Jamey and Hayden, with him to join Carey and cheer me on from the stands.

When the starting gun was fired, I got off to a good start and was leading the field with only a few meters to go when I became aware that the man on my right was almost even with me. I completely forgot my coach's last words of advice, and in the split second I lost my focus, that man beat me by four tenths of one second. Later, Mac said I would have beaten him if my big nose had been a fraction of an inch bigger. I am proud of my silver medal but it still gripes me to know that I would have been the national champion in my very first national meet if that long-legged man from Arizona had just stayed at home. I was disappointed but it was a good learning experience for me. Since then, I have concentrated harder on maintaining my focus without being distracted by anything. It's something that's very hard for me to do and it's something I still have to work on.

That brings me to another major event in the year 2001. On April 22, 2001, our third great granddaughter and sixth great grandchild, Elayna Hammond, was born and immediately took center stage and she has made sure she remained there to this day. Her very protective older brother (by five years), Jessey, has always been very proud of her as has been the whole Hammond clan.

Carey was still hanging in there at the end of the year joyfully cleaning the clocks of all the Minnesota bridge players she could round up.

What a Beautiful Sunset

In honor of Carey's 86th birthday, her sister-in-law, Jane Willis, entertained Carey's bridge club on February 6, 2001. She has been a member of this same bridge club for 22 years. Carey is blowing out her birthday candle.

Carey's bridge club members on her 86th birthday. Standing from left to right: Doris Budd, Vela Dean, Helen Purdy, Liavan Sims, Barbara Norris. Seated left to right: Betty Tillman, Carey and Carol Hotcaveg.

2001

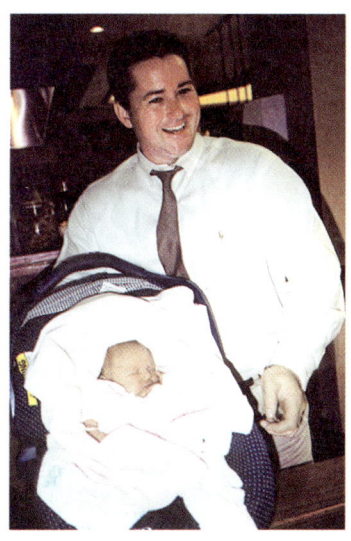

Mac flew down on April 24, 2001, for a one-week R&R visit with us. We flew back to Minneapolis with him and returned home a week later, May 1. Our 6th great grand-child, Elayna Hammond, was born on Sunday, April 22, and we were there on Tuesday, two days later to welcome her into our family. On April 29, at the age of one week, she attended her first family dinner gathering and is pictured here with her proud father, John.

Mac and I as we board Mac's plane for Baton Rouge. Carey, Jim, and his family are already on board.

What a Beautiful Sunset

The National Senior Olympic Games were held in Baton Rouge, LA, July 14-28-2001, in which I competed in the 100-meter run. Pictured from left to right, great granddaughter Hayden, granddaughter-in-law Kristin, grandson Jim, myself and Carey, with great grandson Jamey, peeping over the olympic flag which was furnished by Ann Smith and Betty Dvorak who were at the Valdosta Airport to see us off.

2001

My last assignment before retiring from Allstate on January 1, 1974, was in Baton Rouge, LA. We had always planned to revisit Baton Rouge but it never worked out. Now, 27 years later, I was back in Baton Rouge to compete in the National Senior Olympics. Shortly before leaving Valdosta for Baton Rouge, I called one of my former Baton Rouge agents, Leonard Henry, and told him we'd be there for the Senior Olympic Games. He invited Carey and me, along with Mac and his family, to his home for dinner the evening before my race. When we arrived for the party, we were surprised to find eight of my former Baton Rouge agents and their wives there to welcome us, none of whom had we seen in 27 years. It was a wonderful reunion and all 16 of them were in the stands the next day to cheer me on. To be so far from home, I had quite a cheering section. It was great! I am pictured with these eight men who called themselves "Jim Hammond's Boys." Although most of them were quite young when I knew them, I recognized all except one. Leonard Henry is third from the left in the top row.

What a Beautiful Sunset

Mac with me shortly after the medal award ceremony.

In late October 2001, Jane & Ed Willis gave us a huge farewell party at Langdale Place, inviting all Langdale Place residents and all our close Valdosta friends. Carey is with her sister, Ann.

2001

10A The Valdosta Daily Times

Growing With Our Community

Jim Hammond is 87 years old. He's a grandfather and a great-grandfather. He can run the 100-meter dash in just over 18 seconds. Jim Hammond is a man with an ...

Indomitable WILL

By Dean Poling
dean.poling@gaflnews.com

VALDOSTA

Jim Hammond starts running from the curb of the sidewalk. He starts fast and gains speed along the concrete. He's running specifically for a photograph. I'm holding the camera; he moves fast. I expected a run-walk-trot. Jim Hammond runs flat-out. I watch dumb-founded. He flashes by, legs pumping, without one frame of film shot.

Embarrassed, I ask him if he can run it again for the picture. Jim Hammond smiles; he's not even breathing hard after his dash. His pulse is steady. He walks back to the curb and runs again, runs even faster this time. The camera clicks away as he blurs by.

The second run doesn't wind him either. Jim Hammond is 87 years old, he's a great-grandfather, and I have a different outlook on this thing society calls "old age."

The congratulation poster for his recent second-place victory at the National Senior Olympics hangs above the entrance to Hammond and his wife's hallway to the rooms where they live in Langdale Place. Another poster of congratulations is attached to the door of their apartment.

He displays the silver medal and wears a shirt touting his participation in the Georgia Senior Olympics. A photograph shows a score board flashing his winning time in the 100-meter dash during the National Senior Olympics in Baton Rouge, La. — the board notes that Hammond ran 100 meters in 18.4 seconds. The 85-year-old Arizona man who won first place, beat Hammond by less than a second, with a time just under 18 seconds.

But these things are just window dressing compared to seeing him run, not winded, fast, determined. After his run for the photographs, one of Hammond's neighbors says she wished she had his legs. Hammond replies "you can. It just takes some work."

■

It was the early 1970s, when Hammond's son, Mac, urged his father to exercise. Jim Hammond was in his 50s, but he took his son's advice. He started walking and jogging and made exercise a part of his life.

"If you start young, concentrating on being physically fit, you can improve your older years. You can enjoy them instead of dreading them," Hammond says. "If you have poor health, you can't have fun anyway, no matter your age, but if you have good physical health when you are older, there's no reason that you can't enjoy your later years. The 80s have been some of the best years of my life."

Last year, Hammond heard of the Georgia Senior Olympics. With his love for walking and jogging, he decided to participate. He won the race last September, which earned him a spot in this summer's National Senior Olympics.

He decided to train for the Senior Olympics. He picked up his pace gradually switching from a jog to a run. After nearly seven months of training, he called the Senior Olympic officials; he wanted to know the previous winning time for the 100-meter dash in his age group of 85- to 89-year-old men; it was 18 seconds. "When I first heard 18 seconds, I thought I was beat," Hammond says. "My best time after seven months of training was 22 seconds. I thought there is no way I can ever get down to 18 seconds."

But Hammond still had a few months before the National Senior Olympics, and he was anything but beat.

■

Georgia Senior Olympics officials suggested that Hammond find a coach, someone to

Continued on next page

What a Beautiful Sunset

Continued from previous page
push him and prepare him for his race. Hammond found Bruce Beal, a former track star and a track coach. Beal didn't know Hammond, but after seeing him run and realizing Hammond was serious, Beal agreed to coach Hammond.

Beal created a training regimen for Hammond, which put the 87-year-old on the track running sprints and stretches four days a week. The training schedule placed Hammond in the YMCA, working weights with instructor Lisa Noyes, three days a week.

"Bruce said I needed the weight training to improve my strength throughout my body because when you run," Hammond says, "you don't just use the legs but muscles throughout the body."

Under Beal's guidance, Hammond jogged, warmed-up, skipped, fanny-kicked, a long list of running exercises for the track. "After all that and you're dead," Hammond laughs, "you still have to run and stretch. I can be completely winded, but by the time the stretches are over, I'm fine. So my recovery time was good."

Hammond started seeing his 100-meter time dwindle. He cut his former personal best of 22 seconds to lower times. "Bruce took me to open track meets in Tallahassee," Hammond says. "He wanted me to have more experience competing. The first time I went, my time in the 100-meter dash was 19 seconds. The second was 18.7 seconds. The third was 18.3 seconds.

"I went to the National Senior Olympics with the confidence that I could win something."

Last month, Hammond and 12,000 other senior athletes arrived at the campus of Louisiana State University to compete in 18 different sports, in 800 events, during the National Senior Olympics. An estimated 30,000-35,000 spectators watched the games, including Hammond's wife, son and family.

When Hammond's race started, he quickly took the lead. "You know how they say an athlete has to concentrate to win," Hammond says. "He has to remain focused on his goals without letting anything distract him. When the race started, I had that concentration and was ahead. Then I noticed this long-legged, 85-year-old from Arizona pulling up on me. And I focused too much on him. On the tape, you can actually see me slow down a little and him pull ahead."

Still, Hammond won second place, running 100 meters in 18.4 seconds, a time that many men who are 50 years younger, or more, can envy. He won the silver medal.

The National Senior Olympics' winners circle is like the Olympics — a three-tiered platform with first place standing highest in the center, and second and third place a notch or two lower on each side, respectively.

"They call out your name and where you're from and thousands of people are watching in the stands and when they said my name and Valdosta, Ga., and all of those people cheered, it was a very exciting moment. Something you would never expect to happen to you when you are 87 years old."

The aim of the Senior Olympics is to promote healthy aging. Hammond believes he is a good example of the Senior Olympics' goal.

"It is never too late to start exercising," he says. "Even in old age, you can gain strength if you exercise regularly. I'm proof of that. Walking, jogging, doing some weight exercises, any exercise that requires strength can make for a healthier, older life."

Hammond plans to attend the next National Senior Olympics in 2003, but he will have to qualify from Minneapolis, Minn., where the Hammonds plan to move in September to be closer to their son, grandchildren and great-grandchildren.

In 2003, Hammond will be 89 years old and will likely compete again with the first-place winner from Arizona, who will be 87.

"I don't know if I can beat him," Hammond says. "He's got those long legs. Maybe when I'm in my 90s and in a different age category, I'll win first."

Chapter 9

2002

A Minnesota Dairy Farmer

When Carey and I left Valdosta, Georgia, and moved to Minnesota the day after Thanksgiving 2001, the sun was shining brightly and the temperature was in the low 70s. When we arrived in Minneapolis in the late afternoon of that same day and stepped off the airplane, we were greeted by an arctic, wind-driven snowstorm and a sub-zero temperature. That was not an auspicious welcome for two thin-blooded southern elders! The devil had a trap set for me and I stepped from the plane right into it. I became an instant weather-complainer.

I soon learned that old native Minnesotans are a tough lot who take great pride in their native state and rarely ever complain about its wicked winter weather. Some are very defensive about it.

A few months after we moved into Rose Arbor, a retirement community in Maple Grove, a small group of my fellow residents and I were talking and I made the mistake

What a Beautiful Sunset

of voicing my opinion of the nasty-stinking weather in the presence of one in the group—a tough old, weather-beaten, retired Minnesota dairy farmer from up near the Canadian border. He turned to me and said in a voice as cold and icy as his native land, "We like our climate. It keeps the trash out." If you've never been called a piece of trash, you can't know how it felt to me when all the others in the group smiled real big. Those smiles said to me, "Well, he got his comeuppance."

My first reaction was embarrassment and anger at the old gentleman. However, after the group disbursed, I soon realized that the tough old dairy farmer was right and did me a big favor. I got my comeuppance and it made me realize that an attitude adjustment was in order. He had the nerve to say what I didn't say when transplanted Yankees criticized the south and I wanted to say but didn't, "If you don't like the south, why don't you move back up north? We like it down here." Now the shoe was on the other foot and here I was doing the very thing that irritated me so much when the Yanks did it.

I have always been amazed by the wonder-working power of positive thinking. This was a golden opportunity to put it to a real test. When slapped in the face with a blast of sub-zero arctic air, could I stop complaining and say as well as think, "This is invigorating and I like it," instead of thinking and saying, "This is awful and I hate it?" I decided to give it a try.

Now, after five years of diligent effort, I can say that I don't have to pretend any more. It actually is invigorating and I don't hate it. If the Lord gives me two or three more years on planet Earth, I will be able to look any transplanted southern weather-complainer squarely in the eye and say, without equivocation, "We like our climate. It keeps the trash out," thanks to a wise old Minnesota dairy farmer.

By the end of 2002, our first full year in Minnesota, at age 87 and 88 respectively, Carey and I had made a happy adjustment to our new life here. It took at least a month to recover from the shock of being greeted by a massive blizzard with its wind-driven sleet and snow when we stepped off the plane the day after Thanksgiving 2001. After our recovery from that initial shock, we made it through our first winter with little more than a few muffled weather complaints. The joy of being surrounded by family made it much easier for us to "endure" the harsh winter weather. We missed our Valdosta friends but we made many new ones at Rose Arbor (our retirement community) and at Mac's church.

I've heard it said that the highest taxes in the nation are paid by Minnesota residents. That might be a good thing if Minneapolis is representative of the rest of the state. Everywhere you go in Minneapolis you see evidence that the taxpayers' money is being well spent. When I say Minneapolis, I'm including its many, many beautiful suburbs. There are beautifully maintained parks all over the place, mostly around our hundreds of lakes. There are paved trails for bikers and joggers in all neighborhoods, including downtown. I have yet to see a neighborhood without sidewalks. In early spring, dozens and dozens of crews throughout greater Minneapolis can be seen planting flowers that bloom the entire summer in all the parks, median strips, and other public areas.

What a Beautiful Sunset

Homeowners throughout the area show great pride of ownership and one rarely sees a lawn that isn't manicured to perfection. Parks with picnic areas and great athletic facilities for children's and young adults' summer sports can be found in all the larger neighborhoods. Minnesota summers are relatively short but nowhere, I believe, are they enjoyed more and the public recreational facilities used as much. I love the great outdoors and the beauty of nature in all its form. The beauty of sparkling-clean Minneapolis and the wonderful outdoor summer recreational facilities it provides for its residents make me proud to be a Minnesotan.

The expense to which the city has gone in providing public recreational and sports facilities is amazing. For example, I was astonished when I saw a whole soccer field in Plymouth being enclosed by a huge inflatable dome for use by various winter sports in addition to soccer. The soccer field was even encircled by a track for joggers and track events. Someone told me it cost over 10 million dollars. All these things help make Minneapolis a much better place to live. My hat is off to beautiful Minneapolis, my new home city.

Back to our activities in the year 2002. In June, I won a gold medal in the Minnesota Senior Olympics in the 100-meter run. This qualified me to compete in the National Senior Olympics, which was held in May 2003, in Norfolk, VA. To stay in shape, I continued running and working out on weight machines at my health club five days every week. As for Carey, energy conservation and comfort ranked high on her priority list. She limited her exercise program to walking up and down our hallway to and from the dining room three times daily, and to shifting positions in her recliner as she read and snoozed. It seemed to work quite well for her as she continued to enjoy life and was relatively healthy.

We took three vacations during the year—all with the family. One at Pelican Lake (a two-hour drive north of here) and two at Mac's beach house in Destin, FL, on one of which Carey and I took a four-day side trip to Boca Raton for a wonderful visit with my sister, Nancy. Also, as a special bonus, Carey's brother and sister-in-law, Ed and Jane Willis, from Valdosta, and their daughter, Kathi, and her family from Grand Forks Air Force Base in South Dakota, spent Easter with us.

MY PIMP COAT STORY

Mac's church has a number of very wealthy members, some of whom like to bless him with expensive gifts, things they know or think he likes. A fully equipped fishing boat and a very expensive gun collection are a couple of things that come to mind.

One day I was in Mac's office and noticed this unusual-looking winter coat hanging in his coat closet. I asked Mac about it. He explained that it was left in his office by an anonymous donor with an unsigned note pinned to it that read, "Stay warm. Enjoy." Mac's haberdasher estimated its cost at between $2,500 and $3,000. It had been hanging in that closet for more than a year and he'd never worn it. It was much too showy for him. He doesn't like to call attention to himself. I do. When Mac asked me if I'd like to have it, I took it and left before he had a chance to change his mind. I'd wear anything that cost $3,000, no matter what it looked like, and I loved the way that coat looked.

What a Beautiful Sunset

This is the coat that Mac was given and he gave it to me. I call it my "pimp coat."

That coat is hard to describe but I'll try. The inside and big collar are sheared, honey-colored lamb's wool. The outside has panels of sheepskin leather with each panel being trimmed with strips of the honey-colored lamb's wool.

I had a honey-colored fur Russian cap I wear with it. Every time I go out wearing that coat, it has the effect I'd hoped for. Complete strangers, mostly ladies, look me up and down and make such comments as, "Nice coat!" or, "I like your coat." I loved it.

One day when I was wearing it, I was entering Rose Arbor as Mr. Farr was coming out. Mr. Farr is the owner-operator of the Rose Arbor retirement complex where we live and many other similar operations throughout the Midwest. Very rich! He was wearing a coat like mine except mine is knee length and his was down to his ankles. Now Mr. Farr is a very tall, slender man, about six-feet-six inches, so his coat must have cost twice as much as mine. Very impressive. When he saw my coat, he asked if I had time for a funny story. Of course I did!

It seems there was a complaint from a new ground-floor tenant of one of his new buildings that cold air was coming into her bedroom from around her window. In the middle of a snowstorm while wearing his long coat, Mr.

2002

Farr was outside the lady's bedroom window checking for the leak. She saw him, grabbed her phone, dialed 911 and said, "Come quick! There's a big tall pimp standing outside my bedroom window peeping in at me." Now I know why Mac wouldn't wear that coat. He used good judgment as he's a minister, but I'm not one and I love my pimp coat. If strangers think I'm a pimp, so be it. At least they'll think I'm a very rich one.

Mac had a speaking engagement in Lakeland, Florida over the weekend of April 20, 2002. He, Carey, and I flew to Destin on Monday, April 15 and stayed at his beach house through Thursday the 18th. On Friday the 19th, he flew Carey and me to Boca Raton, dropped us off, flew to Lakeland for his speaking engagement, returned to Boca on Tuesday the 23rd, picked us up, and we flew home. We had a wonderful four-day visit in Boca with my 91-year old sister, Nancy. Since we now live so far apart, both Nancy and I were concerned that at our age something might happen to one of us before we could see each other again, so this visit was extra special. Nancy, Carey, and I are pictured here.

What a Beautiful Sunset

My sister Nancy and I in Boca Raton 2002.

On June 26, 2002, I won a gold medal in the 100-meter run in the Minnesota Senior Olympic Games which were held in Duluth, Minnesota (a four-hour drive north of here). I beat a 70-year-old by a nose.

2002

Joan Costello, our Executive Director at Rose Arbor, and our Head Nurse, Denise Foley, got up at 5 AM and drove to Duluth in time for my race at 9:30 AM, bringing with them "Run, Jim, Run" signs and lots of cheer. You can imagine how much I appreciated their support. They made a big deal of my gold medal upon our return to Rose Arbor. Pictured left to right are Mac, me, Joan, Carey and Denise.

When the girl attempted to drape the gold medal around my neck the ribbon got stuck on my nose. Of course, Mac thought that was hilarious.

What a Beautiful Sunset

On September 15, 2002, at the age of 44, Carey's niece (and therefore mine) Kathi Willis Hunnewell was operated on for pancreatic cancer here in Minneapolis. We call her our "miracle girl" as so few people survive pancreatic cancer. Through her faith and optimistic determination, she beat the odds and survived. She's a very special person and very dear to our whole family. This picture was taken the day after her operation.

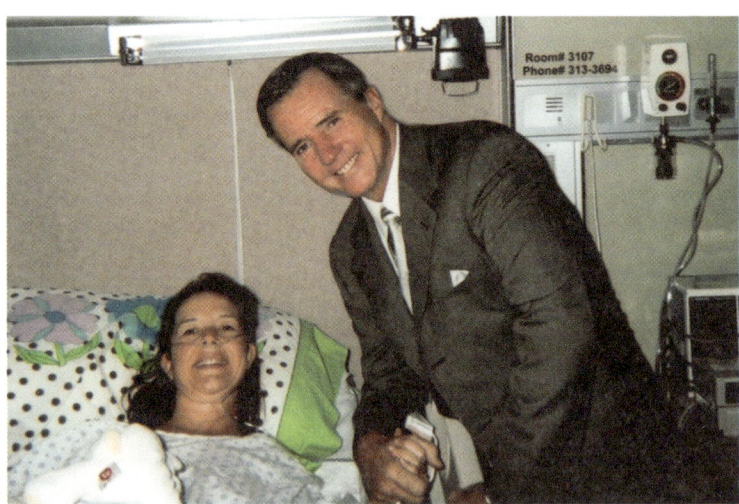

Mac with Kathi the day after her operation.

Chapter 10

2003

On August 12, 2003, for the 23rd time, we moved again. That was a short move—from Maple Grove, MN to Plymouth, MN, an adjoining Minneapolis suburb. Twenty-three moves in 64 years of marriage! That must have set a record for the Hammond clan. We moved into a beautiful third-floor apartment with a gorgeous view of the Minnesota countryside. Our apartment was in one of three buildings in a fabulous, new retirement complex that offered many great amenities to its residents. It was a near-perfect place for folks our age.

When I left my farmland home in Kentucky at the age of 18 and joined the Navy to see the world, I became what might be described as the "happy wanderer" and it seems I will remain one for the rest of my life.

In 1964, the year before our son, Mac, graduated from the Virginia Military Institute and began pilot training at Moody Air Force Base in Valdosta, Georgia, we built a beautiful home in Roanoke, Virginia where I worked for Allstate Insurance Company. We fully expected it to be our retirement home. It was located on the crest of a high ridge that overlooked a deep green ravine or valley, on the other side of which was a towering, tree-covered mountainside. When

What a Beautiful Sunset

I sat on our front porch and drank in that view, my spirit soared with the eagles that nested on that mountainside. There was no doubt in my mind at the time that I could rock away my declining years there on that front porch in total peace and joy.

Thirty-eight years later, there we were in far away Plymouth, Minnesota, getting settled into a new apartment. After leaving Roanoke in 1969, and by the time we landed in Minnesota, we had moved into and out of 12 other houses or apartments located in eight different cities and five different states. Those are pretty amazing moving statistics, but consider this. During our 66 years of marriage, we lived in eight different states and 14 different cities. We lived in 14 different apartments and owned and lived in 10 different homes all of which were brand new with the exception of one that had been lived in. Of the 14 apartments, several were temporary residences while our houses were being built.

I did my own landscaping for each of our nine new homes and I re-landscaped the 10th. For me, it was a labor of love. Our yards were always among the most beautiful in our neighborhoods.

To allay any suspicion that all this is another example of my tendency to inflate the numbers to make a good story, I'll prove with pictures that I'm not guilty and I'll do it by the numbers—House No. 1 thru House No. 10. And for good measure, I'll throw in a picture of our old Kentucky family home where the four youngest family members (George, Nancy, Jeanette, and I) grew up.

Kentucky Home—place where we grew up.

House 1. Brookhaven, GA (Atlanta suburb)
March 1, 1949 – July 1, 1951

What a Beautiful Sunset

House 2. Charlotte, NC
1953 – 1956

House 3. Timberlane Ave., Roanoke, VA
1956 – 1964

House 3. Flower Garden on Timberlane.

House 4. Dogwood Lane, Roanoke, VA
1964 – 1969

What a Beautiful Sunset

House 4. Flower Garden on Dogwood.

House 4. Fountain Garden on Dogwood.

2003

House 5. Juno Isles, Florida
1/1/70 – 12/1/70

House 6. Point Manalapan, Florida
1/1/71 – 12/1/72

House 6. Backyard view of Lake Worth from the swimming pool area of our Point Manalapan home. 1972.

House 7. Baton Rouge, LA
12/1/72 – 12/31/74

House 8. Meridian, Mississippi
1/1/75 – 2/1/79

House 9. Riverhill Drive, Valdosta, Georgia
2/1/79 – 8/1/93

What a Beautiful Sunset

House 9. Flower Garden on Riverhill Dr.

House 10. Georgetown Circle, Valdosta, Georgia
8/1/93 – 8/27/97

2003

Since we loved the people and places everywhere we've lived, can there be a logical explanation for so many moves? Maybe not, but most of those moves were the result of the restless wanderlust that has been surging through my veins since that day I joined the Navy at the age of 18 to see the world. It compels me to always be in pursuit of new challenges, new experiences, new adventures, and new faces, despite my love for the places and faces I leave behind. One would think that my restless wanderlust would subside in my old age, but it has not. Although my home-building days are over, who can say how many more moves my future holds?

Many folks considered our 64-year marriage a major miracle as very few wives would tolerate being uprooted and moved 23 times. One would think Carey would have been unhappy with such a life as she would have loved to live somewhere long enough to put down roots, but she was saved by her easy adaptability, her great disposition, her always happy, positive attitude, and her "what makes Jimmy happy, makes me happy too" approach to our marriage. I thank God for Carey. She was one in a million.

We had a very good year in 2003 except for one devastating experience. I made a disastrous mistake when I ran in the National Senior Olympics in Norfolk, Virginia in May. I wore cleated shoes without having trained in them. They caused me to trip and I took a nosedive. I did it right there in front of all those folks in the stadium, including many friends and relatives who had come to see me win a gold medal! It was awful! I was carted off the field in ignominy and total disgrace on a stretcher, loaded onto an ambulance, and rushed to a hospital.

What a Beautiful Sunset

When I woke up surrounded by Mac, Carey, doctors, and nurses, I wanted to die but now I'm mighty glad I didn't. My injuries were little more than superficial cuts and bruises, but it dealt my once too robust ego a near-fatal blow. Thank goodness, time is a great healer and all my wounds, both physical and psychological, have long since healed.

I soon came to realize that there were positive aspects to my ego-shattering experience. It was certainly a lesson in humility. The response to it on the part of my immediate family, my other relatives, and my good friends, in terms of their love, concern, and understanding, was to me overwhelming. I am now much more acutely aware of the extent to which my life has been blessed and enriched by many great people, both family and good friends. Finally, my efforts to impress everybody with my physical prowess at the ripe old age of 89 was greatly reduced, and that was a very good thing.

I do have one constant reminder of my debacle. My pinkie on my left hand was badly broken and it healed in such a way that it sticks up a bit and then curls down. Now, I'm in high style at fancy tea parties. I didn't stop running and planned to redeem myself by winning the 100-meter sprint in the next National Senior Olympics in May 2005 in Pittsburgh, PA.

On our four-day trip to Norfolk for the senior Olympics, we had a wonderful reunion, before my disastrous fall, with many old Virginia friends. All of us had dinner together and a wonderful visit the evening before my disastrous fall. Among the group were our lifelong friend, Johnny Goodwin, his daughter, Gay, and son, Hobbs, who had driven him down from Richmond to be with us and see me run. That was the first time we had seen Johnny since Alice's death about three years earlier. It was great seeing Johnny but also sad for all of us as we missed Alice. Of course, we didn't realize it then but it was our last visit with Johnny as he died a year later. It's hard to accept the fact that both Alice and Johnny, our best friends for a lifetime, are both gone.

In addition to that trip, we enjoyed two 10-day family vacations at Mac's beach house in Destin, Florida (April and July), two brief visits with my sister, Nancy, in Boca Raton, Florida, a wonderful two-week stay in Valdosta enjoying relatives and friends, and several short trips during the year to the lake house just north of here. Combine all that with our many family activities here at home and you have two very busy and happy, but sometimes frazzled out old folks.

Carey had a very painful knee (arthritis) that made it difficult for her to walk but she never once let it limit her activities and never complained about her pain. We celebrated our 64th wedding anniversary on December 31.

July 2003, Jim and Kristin shortly before they and their children left for a two-year stay in Singapore.

What a Beautiful Sunset

The rise and fall of a runner

BY RHODA FUKUSHIMA
Pioneer Press

Jim Hammond

Shortly before he retired, insurance executive Jim Hammond began jogging and working out at a YMCA in Georgia, where he lived at the time. Someone there suggested he try out for the state Senior Olympics. He was 85.

Though he has macular degeneration, Hammond decided to compete, and he won a gold medal. Later, he hired a coach and dropped his time in the 100-meter dash from 30 seconds to just over 18 seconds. He won a silver medal at the 2001 national games, only 0.6 seconds behind the winner.

After moving to Maple Grove, Hammond, now 89, kept training and qualified for the 2003 national Senior Olympics. That day, his family and friends came out to watch him run.

"I was so confident that I was going to win a gold medal. You run faster if you have cleated shoes, but they're very risky. If you drag your feet, it pitches you forward. I was so sure I could concentrate on lifting my feet. Being cocky, I wore the cleats without having trained in them.

"I got off to a good start. I was leading the pack. I (must have) let one foot drag. It pitched me forward, and I landed on my face, nose, cheek and forehead. I remember nothing from the time I fell until the time I found myself on a gurney.

"They thought I had a concussion. I had nothing worse than a broken little finger, and superficial cuts on my face that made me look like I'd been through a meat grinder.

"My son said, 'Isn't it a blessing that you have a big nose to cushion you from a concussion?' Had I not been in wonderful physical condition, I would have had multiple broken bones.

"I have a lot of false ego. My ego suffered a near-fatal blow. I was totally disgraced. Can you imagine my humiliation? It was awful.

"After I got home, I sent everybody an e-mail explaining briefly what happened. The outpouring of calls and letters was overwhelming. It made it so much easier.

"Now, my face is completely cleared up. The sun has begun to shine again. I'm recovering fine.

"Most people my age would take that as a clear warning to stop running. People up here, after they saw my face, think I am absolutely nuts to run again.

"But I'm going to run until I win the national Senior Olympics. Next year, I'll be 90 — the youngest in my age group. I should be able to take that even if I run slowly. I might even win by default.

"I took away a lesson in humility. I'm so grateful for all the good friends I have — who love me just as much as they did before. I'll never be as cocky and self-assured.

"It was a humiliating but humbling experience. (Before the race) my son told me at least three times not to wear cleats. He hasn't told me once, 'I told you so.' "

"I guess I needed to come down a few notches. But I didn't have to come down so many. I enjoy life. You can't enjoy life without a good sense of humor. You can't enjoy old age — any age — without good health."

What a Beautiful Sunset

Turning

For five years, people have told us their life-changing stories, and we were impressed by their resilience, determination and hard work. Here are some updates.

Monday, December 29, 2003

Jim Hammond

BY RHODA FUKUSHIMA
Pioneer Press

2003 marked the five-year anniversary of Turning Point.

Since 1998, hundreds of you have shared how you turned the corner toward better health. In the beginning, many stories focused on the body, with perennially popular topics like losing weight and getting stronger. But with time and age, your definition of fitness has broadened. For many of you, it's about being well on all fronts —

Points

TRAINING FOR TRACK

Jim Hammond of Plymouth recovered nicely from the nasty spill he took — while wearing untested cleats — at the 2003 national Senior Olympics. Hammond is back in training, his eyes on the next state and national Senior Olympics. Hammond will be 90 in April.

"I survived my fall in good shape. Time heals everything. My wounded ego is totally recovered.

"I continue to work out. I r un for 30 minutes Monday through Friday. I follow the same schedule that my coach set up for me. After that, I go to the fitness center for about an hour to work on the weight machines. One day, I exercsie all my upper-body muscles. The next day, the lower body. It keeps all my joints and muscles from stiffening up.

"I'm keeping in good shape so I can win the track meet in Duluth next June, the Northland Senior Olympics for the state of Minnesota. If I win that, I'll be qualified to compete in the National Senior Olympics in 2005. I'll be 91 then. I'm just hoping that I'll still be able to run.

"I'll be running the 100-meter sprint. I won't wear cleats. I'll just run as fast as I can — and try to keep up with those who are younger.

"I watch my diet. I eat dessert every night. I eat a lot of fruits and vegetables and very few things with saturated fats. I am 5-foot-8 and weigh 148. My cholesterol is 140. My resting pulse is betweeen 50-55. My blood pressure is 110/65.

"If you feel well, you can enjoy life. I couldn't have asked my 80s to have been a better time in my life. My wife and I will be celebrating our 64th wedding anniversary on New Year's Eve."

What a Beautiful Sunset

These are the fish we caught when we went back-bay fishing on July 6, 2003. Seven-year-old Jessey caught the largest one. A nearby restaurant cooked them to our individual orders. They were great. In the picture, I am standing behind Jessey and Mac. John and the top of Elayna's head are on the left. Two-year-old Elayna didn't go fishing with us but she and Beckey were on the dock to meet us upon our triumphal return.

We said "goodbye" to 2003 and "hello" to 2004 while on a great visit with friends and relatives in Valdosta (December 30–January 10). We celebrated our 64th wedding anniversary on December 31, 2003, at a dinner hosted by Carey's brother and sister-in-law, Ed and Jane Willis at the Valdosta Country Club. In the picture seated around the table from left to right are Ed, his son, Al Willis, Carey's brother-in-law, Charlie Aldridge, Carey's sister, Ann, myself, Carey, and Jane.

Chapter 11

2004

My 90th birthday was on Monday, April 5, 2004. It was celebrated at five different birthday dinner parties, with a birthday cake at each, in three different states, all in a six-day period. Sounds ridiculous, doesn't it? Since some may suspect that I still exaggerate at age 90, I have pictures to prove it. That should break some kind of record for a 90th birthday.

Birthday Party No. 1: It was on April 4, the day before my birthday. Two very special friends of ours, Joan Costello and Denise Foley, told Carey and me to dress up in our finest as they wanted us to be their guests at a birthday dinner party at one of Minneapolis' finest restaurants. When they picked us up, they pinned a red-rose boutonniere on my coat lapel and a corsage on Carey's shoulder. The table was decorated with flowers, balloons, and beautifully wrapped presents. After a delicious dinner, the whole serving staff marched to our table with a beautiful birthday cake, singing "Happy Birthday" with the whole restaurant joining in. Someone must have told them how I love being in the limelight. They sure knew how to melt my 90-year-old heart and make it sing.

Birthday Party No. 2: On my birthday, Monday, April 5, Mac and Lynne hosted a beautiful party with lots of fun, presents, and love. It was attended by our whole family and a number of our special friends.

Birthday Party No. 3: Mac had a speaking engagement in Lakeland, Florida on Wednesday, April 7. On Tuesday, he flew Carey and me to Boca Raton, dropped us off in Boca Raton and flew up to Lakeland for his speaking engagement the next day. We had a wonderful visit Tuesday night and all day Wednesday with my beloved 93-year-old sister, Nancy. Wednesday evening, Nancy and her two Florida daughters, Jean and Martha, took us out for a birthday dinner and my third birthday cake.

Birthday Party No. 4: Mac flew down from Lakeland Thursday morning, picked us up and we flew to Bowling Green, Kentucky. My great niece, Amy Wood, met us at the airport, drove us to her home where we had lunch with her family. That afternoon, she drove us to Franklin, Kentucky (21 miles). That evening, my niece, Nancy Carol, hosted a huge dinner party—a combination birthday and family reunion (all my Kentucky kin). I love family reunions and this one was great. My fourth birthday cake!

Birthday Party No. 5: Another combination deal and not really a birthday party for me but I'm counting it as one since I was served my fifth birthday cake. It was a reunion for everyone who graduated from Middleton High School in or before 1940 (over 100 of us attended). I graduated in 1932 so it was the 72nd anniversary of my graduation and I outranked everyone there in terms of age. I was the speaker for the evening and they sang "Happy Birthday" to me. It's on that basis and the cake that I'm claiming it as my "Birthday Party No. 5." I admit it's quite a stretch but by admitting it, I'm hoping Carey will forgive me.

We flew home to Minneapolis Saturday morning and didn't know we were exhausted until we got there. The adrenalin flow and all the excitement had kept us going. I do believe that Carey withstood that whirlwind of events and travel better than I and enjoyed it as much as I did.

To be so old, we really stayed on the move throughout the year and covered a lot of ground. In addition to the foregoing, we visited friends and relatives in Valdosta, GA, I ran in the state senior Olympics in Duluth and won two gold medals, we vacationed at the beach in Destin, FL, and made several trips with Mac to beautiful Pelican Lake in northern Minnesota for short three-to-five day visits.

For the most part, my life revolved around the senior Olympics and the rigorous exercise routine I follow. I spend from 9 AM to noon, five days a week, at the track running and at a fitness center working out. It's something I love doing, but more importantly, it pays big dividends. It keeps me physically fit and has extended my good health into my 90s. My participation in the Senior Olympics and the medals I have won give me a sense of accomplishment and bring me more fun and excitement in my old age than I dreamed possible.

Carey's enthusiasm and enjoyment of life did not wane during the year despite her increasingly painful knee, but help was on the way. She had knee-replacement surgery on December 6. After a six-week recovery and rehab period, she had less pain but still had to use a walker.

What a Beautiful Sunset

I was 90 years old on April 5, 2004. This picture of Nancy and me was taken on April 27, 2004 shortly before our departure for Kentucky. Nancy asked me if I remembered that we always locked our little fingers when we were children when one swore the other to secrecy. I did remember. Note that our little fingers are locked in this picture.

The first of four 90th birthday parties hosted by good friends, Joan Costello and Denise Foley.

My first 90th birthday cake.

April 27, 2004. Pictured above are my Kentucky relatives who joined me at the home of my niece, Nancy Carol Guthrie, for my third 90th birthday party. In the back row is my great niece, Amy Hughes Wood, her father Tommy Hughes, Mac, my niece Nancy Carol Guthrie, my great nephew Joe Boyd Hammond, my nephew Ben Proctor Linton and his wife Ginger, my great-great nephew Andrew Wood (Amy's son), and Scott Guthrie (Nancy Carol's husband). Middle row: Me, Carey, Nancy Carol's and Scott's twin daughters Jo and Jamey Guthrie (I can't tell them apart) and their dog. Bottom row: Amy's youngest son—my great-great nephew Paul Wood, Joe Boyd Hammond's two sons—my great-great nephews, and last but not least, my 96-year-old high school teacher and lifetime family friend, Edessa Chapman Thurmond.

What a Beautiful Sunset

April 27, 2004. Scott looks on while I talk to his and Nancy Carol's son, Jason, who called from Texas to wish me a happy birthday.

April 28, 2004. I am greeting Rev. James R. Banton. He and Lillian Oslin Stamps are my only surviving classmates. Lillian was unable to attend.

2004

I am blowing out the candles on my birthday cake while Carey looks on.

I am pictured with John and Rebecca Shugart Searcy. Although Rebecca is a few years younger than I, we grew up together and her parents, Mr. Tom and Miss Eula May Shugart, owned and operated Middleton's only general merchandise store. In fact, it was the only store of any kind in Middleton and the rocking chairs across its front porch were always filled with "old cronies" every Saturday afternoon.

What a Beautiful Sunset

NORTHLAND SENIOR GAMES
Newsletter

Let us tell you just a few stories about participants from the 2004 games. Consider James Hammond, a 90 year old from Minnesota who ran the 100 meter in track and field. At the 2001 Nationals at the age of 87, he won a silver medal, losing by .6 seconds to an 85 year old from Arizona. Legally blind, he then again qualified at the state level in 2002 and went on to Nationals in Hampton Roads, Virginia last year to pursue his dream of winning a gold medal at the national level. Deciding to wear cleats at the last minute in the hopes of getting a faster time, he instead tripped and fell on the track, ending up in the emergency room of a local hospital. After the healing of his wounded body and bruised ego, he redeemed himself in June. Coming into the Northland Senior Games, his fastest time was 18.3 seconds and he went home with a gold medal and a time of 19.5. We are confident that his tremendous spirit, clever sense of humor, and determination will take him to that of a National Senior Games gold medalist, and at last report, he even had his eye on breaking the international record in his age division!

THE PHENOM

After starting competitive running at 86, James Hammond has set several national age group records

RunMinnesota RECENTLY INTERVIEWED 90 year old track star, James Hammond, about his background and training for the 2005 Senior Olympics this June in Pittsburgh. Hammond, although fairly new to running, having started at the age of 86, has his sights set on National and World records in the 100 meter and 400 meter sprint events at the upcoming games.

RUNMINNESOTA: Where are you from?

James Hammond: I am a native born Kentuckian and lived in Valdosta, Georgia for 23 years before my wife and I moved to Minneapolis three years ago to be near our family. We now live within an eight mile radius of our son, daughter-in-law, three grandchildren and six great grandchildren.

RM: What got you started running? What is your athletic background?

JH: I have always been very active and have jogged and worked out spasmodically for many years. I celebrated my ninetieth birthday on April 5, 2004, and I did not begin running and working out on a regular basis until the fall of 2000 when I was 86 years old. I entered the Georgia Golden Olympics in August 2000. I did so without ever in my life having competed in any sports event, other than golf. I won a gold medal in the 100 meter run without any prior training. Eight months later, I had reduced my running time for the 100 meter sprint from 30 seconds to 23 seconds and that seemed the best I could do.

I thought that was pretty good, until I checked with Vicki Pilgrim, a Georgia Golden Olympics official, and she told me that all national winners in my age group (85-89) in prior years had done it in 18 to 19 seconds. I will always be grateful to Vicki, as I was ready to throw in the towel until she insisted that I find a track coach to help me. I found a good one who pushed me to my limit on

Continued on next page

Continued from previous page

both the track and in the gym on weights. Three months later I was headed for Baton Rouge and the National Senior Olympics and ran second place in 18.4 to the first place, all-time, new national record of 17.6 seconds.

RM: Any recent competitions?

JH: In November 2001, my wife and I moved to Minneapolis. I began running and working out on weights five to six days each week following the exercise routine my Georgia coach had laid out for me. I had seven months to prepare for the Minnesota Northland Senior Olympics which were held in Duluth in June 2002. I won the 100 meter gold medal, which qualified me to compete in the National Senior Olympics in June 2003 in Hampton Roads, Virginia.

> It's hard to believe, but my 80s were among the happiest and most rewarding years of my life and my participation in the Senior Olympics has played a hugely important role in making it so. The hard work and rigorous exercise routine I have had to follow in order to excel have paid off big time.

In Virginia, I made one fatal mistake. I was told shortly before leaving that one gets better traction and can run faster in shoes with cleats. So, without having trained in them, I wore cleated shoes. I got off to a great start and was leading the pack with a national gold squarely in my sights when the cleats on my left shoe scraped the rubberized surface of the track and vaulted me high into the air. I made a perfect, head-first, three-point landing on my nose, left cheek and forehead right there in front of a stand full of stunned, horrified people, including all my friends and relatives who had come to see me win a gold medal. I knew I couldn't quit and had to redeem myself.

I made a determined resolve then and there to do whatever might be necessary to win a national gold medal at my first opportunity. I immediately began preparing for the first hurdle. A gold medal in the Minnesota Senior Olympics in June 2004. To increase my challenge, I decided to compete in both the 100 meter and the 400 meter runs. I won gold medals in both. My running time in each was faster than the existing national records. I ran the 400 meter race in 1:54 and the 100 meters in 19.5 seconds.

RM: What are your goals for Pittsburgh?

JH: I decided to seek professional help to enhance my chances of increasing my speed and endurance, and I found Bob Dahl, a trainer at Lifetime Fitness Center. I wasted no time engaging his services as my running coach. I am overwhelmed and astounded by the results I have achieved under his tutelage in such a short time. I can now run 100 meters in 17.3 to 18.1. I now average running 400 meters in about 1:51 seconds, so I still have some work to do on my endurance.

My goal has been to break both national records, but after Bob worked such a miracle for me, I have upgraded my goal and I now plan to break both world records. The very thought of the possibility of my becoming a world champion senior athlete almost blows what's left of my 90-year-old mind.

When I fell at the 2003 national games, a local newspaper wrote a story about me and entitled it, "The Rise and Fall of a Runner." If I break the world record, I plan to insist that the newspaper write a sequel entitled, "Hark! The Fallen Runner Has Arisen."

RM: Anything else you would like to share with us?

JH: It's hard to believe, but my 80s were among the happiest and most rewarding years of my life and my participation in the Senior Olympics has played a hugely important role in making it so. The hard work and rigorous exercise routine I have had to follow in order to excel have paid off big time. Aside from the joy of winning a number of medals, there's no doubt in my mind that my hard work and strenuous exercise are largely responsible for the extension of my near perfect health into my 90s.

Of almost equal importance, my participation in the Senior Olympics has brought me a level of fun and excitement in my old age that I never dreamed possible. And now, with the prospect of breaking a world record this year in Pittsburgh, it appears that my 90s will be just as much fun as my 80s.

If any athletes or anyone else who dreads old age read this, I hope they'll listen up and take heed to the advice of this old pro. Don't wait until a disabling health problem strikes. Begin exercising hard and regularly and eating sensibly right now while you are in good health. If you stay healthy, there should be no reason to dread old age. It can be a great time to live it up, have fun, and enjoy life to the hilt.

At first, following a demanding, regular workout routine five days a week required considerable self-discipline, but I soon came to love it and now feel cheated if anything interferes. The Senior Olympics program offers an opportunity to everyone age 50 and up, to enjoy actual participation in their favorite sport or sports for the rest of their lives. It has been good for my mind, body, and soul, and I never expect to experience the loneliness and boredom that plague so many old folks.

Chapter 12

2005

In our 80s, we were octogenarians. When both of us got to be in our 90s, I didn't know what we were. Even though I didn't know the word for it, I did know its definition—REALLY old.

First off, we enjoyed a wonderful, elaborate celebration of Carey's 90th birthday on February 6 with our whole family. Carey was radiant and positively glowed when showered with all the love, attention, and stack of beautifully wrapped birthday presents.

The very next day, we headed south for Valdosta, Georgia for a three-month stay. We rented an apartment in our former retirement complex, Langdale Place. It was nice to escape part of Minnesota's winter weather but even nicer to be with our many great Valdosta friends.

When we got home on April 15, a lot of hard training lay ahead of me as less than two months remained until I participated in the National Senior Olympics in Pittsburgh, June 6-10. However, with the help of a good coach and a lot of hard work, I was ready. I won two gold medals and broke the all-time national records in my age group (90–94, I was 91) in the 100 and 400-meter runs. But wonders didn't cease there. Cable television's sports network, ESPN, did a documentary on me and it aired in February. To say that I enjoyed all the notoriety that went with being featured in a story on national television is the understatement of the year.

On June 29, Carey and I, along with several members of our family, took part in an historic event. Carey joined Bethel Baptist Church, Midland, GA, a Columbus suburb, when she was 11 years old and was baptized in nearby Flat Rock Creek. The church was founded 180 years ago and her great grandfather, Carey Curry Willis, was its first member. He was ordained a minister in 1840 and was its pastor for 54 years until his death in 1894. As the great-great grandson of the church's most illustrious pastor, Mac was invited to preach the 180th anniversary celebration sermon. We flew down with him for the big event. Mac's message was beautiful and absolutely perfect for the occasion. Carey and I were very proud of him. For a family history buff like me, it was an awe-inspiring experience. Immediately following the services, we flew to Destin, Florida for a two-week family vacation. What a perfect place to relax, unwind, and enjoy the golden sunshine on a beautiful beach with its pure-white sand!

In the last half of the year, most of our activities revolved around church and family affairs, all of which we enjoyed. However, for me, not one of them matched the fun and excitement of winning gold medals and breaking national records. Of course, being featured in a story about me on national TV was no small deal for a publicity loving hound like me.

2005

February 6, 2005, Carey's 90th birthday party attended by family (except for Jim's—they were still in Singapore) and a few of our friends from SummerWood. Russ Lofgren, Jr. is escorting Carey into the dining room where guests are waiting.

Carey's 90th birthday party continues. Mac and I are standing behind Carey before dinner is served.

What a Beautiful Sunset

This picture is of Hayden with me showing off both my gold medals which was taken in Pittsburgh Friday morning shortly before we headed home after my 400-meter race.

On the plane headed for home.

REPRINT

91-year-old wins gold at Olympics
Thursday, June 23, 2005

He's 91, and he's still running.

Simpson County native James Hammond recently won two gold medals and broke two national records for his age group (90-94) at the 2005 National Senior Olympics held in Pittsburgh, Pa.

Hammond won the 100- and 400-meter runs. In addition to capturing the gold medals, he also broke the official all-time national records in both events for the 90-94-year-old age group. Hammond won the 100-meter event by two seconds and captured the 400-meter event by 18 seconds. In both events, he beat former national record holders.

At age 91, James Hammond won two gold medals and broke two national records at the 2005 National Senior Olympics.

However, he fell just short of setting new world records.

"My initial reaction was bitter disappointment as my heart was set on breaking the world records, and I didn't," said Hammond. "You see, I consistently beat the world record in my practice sessions. When it finally sank in that I can run both 100 and 400 meters faster than any man in the whole United States in my age group, my earlier disappointment turned into wild elation."

Hammond is a graduate of the old Middleton High School in west Simpson County and was one of the speakers at the school's reunion last year. He now lives in Minnesota.

The cable television sports network ESPN is doing a documentary on Hammond's life. A film crew from ESPN spent a day with Hammond

Continued on next page

REPRINT

What a Beautiful Sunset

REPRINT

Continued from previous page
just prior to the National Senior Olympics, filming his regular workout routine along with conducting interviews with Hammond and his family. The crew then went to Pittsburgh to film Hammond's performance at the National Senior Olympics.

Hammond says he will rest a while before preparing for the next National Senior Olympics scheduled for June 2007 in Louisville.

"It's time for me to rest up a bit before beginning my training for the next National Senior Olympics … Clear the track. Here comes the national champion running for the roses in good old Derby Town and a shot at the world title," said Hammond. "It might be best that I didn't break the world record as it might motivate me to keep on working hard to break it in the nationals in 2007." **FF**

REPRINT

Bethel Baptist Church, Midland, Georgia. On June 29, 2005, Mac, Lynne, John and Beckey and their two children (Jessey and Elayna) and Carey and I took part in an historic event in Midland, Georgia—the celebration of the 180th anniversary of the founding of Bethel Baptist Church.

Chapter 13

2006

In 2005, we spent February 7 to April 15 in Valdosta. It was so nice and Carey had such a wonderful time with her old bridge buddies that we decided to spend January, February, and March down there in 2006. Another incentive for staying longer was the fact that Carey's arthritis bothered her much less in the warmer climate.

We left Minnesota the day after Christmas and flew to Destin with Mac and Lynne where we spent a week at the beach before flying to Valdosta on January 2. It was even better than the year before. Our friends, and especially Carey's bridge friends, rolled out the red welcome carpet in a big way. There were few days, between January 2 and her fatal fall on January 27, that she wasn't honored by a table of bridge or a big bridge party.

Two good friends of ours, Sybil Mashburn of Atlanta and Gracelee Quillian of Charleston, paid us a three-day visit in Valdosta. Gracelee flew to Atlanta, joined Sybil and they drove down, arriving late Wednesday afternoon, January 25, and left very early Saturday morning, January 28. On Friday, January 27, we had a party and invited 47 of our good old Valdosta friends to meet our guests and help us celebrate our more than 60-year friendship with these two very special ladies. Before describing this fateful party, I'm going to digress and tell the story of this long friendship. It's a long but quite interesting story and I hope you will enjoy reading it.

Way back in the mid-40s when I headed Delta Airlines' Charleston, South Carolina office, a beautiful, young, South Carolina country girl named Sybil Moore applied for a job with Delta. I have always loved pretty faces and I must admit that I was impressed by the natural beauty of this little country girl who was born with more than her share of it. I am proud that, aside from her beauty, I sensed her sharp intellect, her thirst for knowledge, her determination to better her lot in life, and her great potential. I hired her on the spot despite her lack of qualifications in terms of experience and a college education. I'm happy to say that she more than justified my faith in her.

Four years later, she married my boss, Charlie Mashburn, and I am proud that I was the matchmaker who brought them together. I'm also glad I was at the wedding as Charlie's best man and helped tie the knot so securely that it never came untied. Despite Charlie's having been born with a silver spoon in his mouth, he was one of the most self-effacing and most unpretentious people I have ever known—a really good man and a devout Christian. He came from a well-to-do, old Atlanta family, his father being a prominent Atlanta physician.

In her role as the wife of a successful, young businessman, it was fascinating to watch Sybil's quick, Pygmalion-like (somewhat of a stretch) transformation from a South Carolina country girl to a charming, sophisticated, and stunning-looking southern lady, who was capable of charming any group. Unlike the storybook Pygmalion, Sybil did it on her own with little help from others. She was as natural and unpretentious as Charlie.

Those Charleston Delta employees not only loved their company, their jobs, and their fellow employees and working together, they loved playing together. The first summer we were there, all the employees chipped in and rented a cottage at Folly Beach and named it the "Delta Shelter." Believe me, a lot of shaking, rattling, rocking and rolling went on there every weekend. Charleston was a layover point for the flight crews so we included the layover pilots and stewardesses at our Delta Shelter parties every weekend. Our Delta Shelter became known to all the flight crews throughout the system and they vied for the weekend Charleston runs.

By this time, Sybil had joined Gracelee Mason as the co-favorite employees of Delta's Charleston operation. That was the beginning of a strong, sister-like relationship between the two of them. It has lasted for the balance of their lives and has become even stronger as they've become older. Grace and Sybil were the "life of the party" at those Delta Shelter gatherings.

If you are anywhere close to my age, you'll remember a beautiful and very popular singer in the 40s and 50s named Patty Page. Sybil looked very much like Patty Page and could sing almost as well. At some point in every Delta Shelter weekend, Sybil was always called on to sing. Being a born ham, she loved it and never refused to entertain us. She sang all the popular songs of that day, but one little ditty in her repertoire invariably brought the house down. It was called *The Persian Kitty*. In those days, it might have been considered a bit naughty but certainly not now. Whenever I think back on those Delta days and Sybil, *The Persian Kitty* always comes to mind. For me, the Delta Shelter, Sybil, and *The Persian Kitty* have become almost synonymous.

Now about Gracelee Mason Quillian. When I was transferred from Atlanta to Charleston in November 1945, she was already working in our Charleston office as a reservations agent. She was a native Charlestonian and I loved her Charleston accent and I do to this day. She was an easy person to love and most everyone who knew her did. She was as friendly and lovable as a little puppy and her happy, enthusiastic, and loving disposition endeared her to her fellow employees and to everyone who knew her.

I had a close friend in Atlanta, Gene Quillian, whose personality and happy outlook on life matched Gracelee's. I felt they were just right for each other. After all, I found a good husband for Sybil, so why not find one for Gracelee. I invited Gene over for a weekend visit and introduced him to Gracelee. It worked just like I hoped it would. A few years later, Gracelee Mason became Mrs. Eugene Quillian. Gene stayed in the service after the war and became a career U. S. Army officer.

When I left Delta in 1949 and went to work for Allstate Insurance Company, my job involved frequent transfers and during my 26-year career with Allstate, we lived in seven different southern states. We eventually lost track of Gene and Gracelee as they were stationed at many different bases around the world before he retired as a full colonel.

Sybil left Charleston and moved to Atlanta when she married and lived there throughout her marriage. We kept in touch with them as I was in and out of Atlanta frequently on business throughout my Allstate career. We had many friends in Atlanta and Carey often accompanied me on these trips. She visited friends while I was at work.

One Sunday in January 1997, I was browsing through an old photograph album covering our Delta days in Charleston and came across a picture of Gracelee and Gene. It brought back a flood of memories of those fun times back there in the days of our youth. I wondered if they had settled in Charleston after Gene's retirement. On an impulse, I picked up the phone, and with the help of directory assistance, I found a listing for Eugene Quillian.

When Grace answered the phone, I recognized her voice immediately as she had lost none of her beautiful Charleston accent. There followed a wonderful one-hour-phone reunion. Lost time seemed to melt away and it was as if there'd never been an interruption in our friendship.

When Gene retired somewhere around 1980, they built a home on James Island in Charleston next door to good friends, Bill and Nelie Thomas, who were also friends of ours from our Charleston Delta days. Bill worked for me as a reservations agent during my two-year tour of duty in Charleston. We had lost track of them too.

In our conversation, Grace told me that they, the Thomas's and the Mashburn's were going on a Caribbean cruise in April and insisted that we join them. I told her we couldn't as we had just returned a week earlier from a cruise-ship tour of the Hawaiian Islands. When I hung up and told Carey about it, she told me to call Gracelee right back and tell her we'd go and that's what I did. Gracelee was elated and suggested we surprise the Mashburn's.

The plan was that we'd go directly to our stateroom when we boarded the ship and lay low until dinner time.

What a Beautiful Sunset

We were to enter the dining room late, find their table and pretend that it was a total coincidence. It worked! When we spotted their table and walked toward it, I heard Sybil say, "That man looks exactly like Jim Hammond," and then screamed, "It is Jim and Carey Hammond." Everybody in that huge dining room turned to see what all the commotion was about. What a reunion! It was as if we had turned back the clock 50 years and were partying again at the Delta Shelter. We had been on many cruises with good friends but that one had to rank at or near the top.

Two years later, in 1999, we had reservations for another Caribbean cruise with the same group, but at the very last minute, the Mashburn's had to cancel due to a medical emergency. Everyone involved was extremely disappointed. Even though this was another great cruise, we missed the Mashburn's terribly. One year later, in 2000, Gene died and about a year ago Sybil lost Charlie. Now they are both widows and I thank God they have each other to lean on for comfort, support, and companionship.

I have thoroughly enjoyed writing this little history of our long friendship with these two lovely ladies. It was great remembering and reliving a great period of time in our lives. This brings us right back to where it started—Carey's last party.

Our 10 AM party was a brunch with beautifully displayed party food and beverages. It was held in the Rose Room at Langdale Place. It is a beautiful room used for large parties and receptions. Carey was in her glory greeting and being loved on by 47 of our good Valdosta friends, including almost every one of her old, beloved bridge friends.

The night before our party, I said to Sybil, "I wish I could hear you sing *The Persian Kitty* one more time before

I die. Is there the slightest possibility that you'd consider singing it at our party tomorrow?" I was amazed and delighted when she, without hesitation, said she'd be happy to. Can you imagine a lady in her late 70s, a non-professional singer, having the nerve, poise, and self-confidence to sing to a room full of total strangers?

After introducing Gracelee and Sybil and giving a little background history of our friendship, I turned the mike over to Sybil. Well, she simply wowed them! I thought they'd never stop applauding.

Here are the words to *The Persian Kitty* that Sybil always rendered with such great éclat.

SYBIL'S PERSIAN KITTY SONG

The Persian kitty, perfumed and fair,
   went out to the garden to get some air.
A tomcat lean, lean and long,
   dirty and yellow came along.
He sniffed at the perfumed Persian cat
   as she walked around with much éclat.
Thinking a bit of time to pass,
   he whispered, oh kid, you sure got class.
It's fitting, it's proper was her reply,
   as she arched her whiskers over her eye.
I'm ribboned and sleep on pillows of silk
   and daily I'm fed on certified milk.
Oh I should be happy with all that I've got,
   but happy I'm not.
Oh I should be happy, happy indeed,
   for I am highly pedigreed.
Cheer up, said the tomcat with a smile

> *and trust your newfound friend for a while.*
> *You needn't escape from the backyard fence.*
> *My dear, all you need is experience.*
> *The morning after the night before,*
>   *when Kitty came home at the hour of four,*
> *the innocent look from her eye had went.*
>   *The smile on her face was a smile of content.*
> *In later years, when neighbors came,*
>   *to see the kittens of pedigreed fame,*
>   *they weren't Persian. They were black and*
> *tan, and she told them their father was a*
> *traveling man – a snatching, scratching*
> *traveling man.*

I have a DVD of the story about me and my senior Olympic running career that was broadcast nationally on ESPN's show called "Timeless." After plenty of time for visiting following Sybil's performance, I played my ESPN DVD. The response it received in terms of applause, as well as comments, almost equaled that which was accorded Sybil's performance. It was a wonderful day for both Carey and me but most especially for Carey. There was no warning of the tragic turn of event later that day.

Sybil and Grace spent the afternoon and early evening with us. They left for their motel immediately after dinner as they had to leave early the next morning. Soon after they left, I went to another room to check my e-mail and Carey went to our bedroom to undress. She was still wearing her party dress. A few minutes later, I heard a loud thump and knew she had fallen. I rushed in and found her lying on the floor in a pool of blood. When she fell, she struck the back of her head on the sharp corner of a bedside table.

The ambulance and paramedics were there in a matter of minutes and she was rushed to the hospital.

She struck the table with such force that it ruptured a blood vessel inside her head and the doctors were not able to stop the slow seepage of blood into her brain. The resulting swelling put pressure on her brain and caused her to sleep almost all the time.

When she was awake, she was completely lucid and her quick wit and good sense of humor showed through each time she was awake, right to her last conscious moment. She said so many clever and funny things over the six-week period she was in the hospital that I can't begin to remember all of them. I regret that we did not write them down while they were fresh in our memories. I would like to repeat a few that I do remember. These remarks were made at various times during that six-week span of time in her wakeful moments. Once when her nurse was testing her alertness, she pointed to me and asked, "Do you know who that is?" She looked at me and said, "Of course I do. He's my lover." Once when I told her I loved her, she said, "Well, you'd darn sure better." Another time, when she woke up and I knew she recognized me, I leaned over, and kissed her on her lips. She said, "Ed (her brother), check my blood pressure. I think it just went through the roof."

One of the last completely audible things she said was her response when I told her I loved her. In a weak but clear whisper she said, "Isn't that interesting, I was just thinking how much I love you." It's incredible to me and the rest of my family that she could think so clearly and make such remarks during the brief moments she was awake, almost to the very end.

What a Beautiful Sunset

She never complained once and not once did she admit to any pain. She was happy, loving, and at peace with herself right to the end. She died the way she lived—happy and with a heart full of unconditional love. No one has ever been better prepared for heaven than my Carey.

Isn't it wonderful that the Lord arranged to have Carey surrounded by her beloved friends at her glorious but fateful farewell party? And who but the Lord could have known that it was her farewell party and that exactly six weeks later to the day, on March 10, 2006, she would be taken to her heavenly home so soon?

Carey died at 11:39 PM, Friday, March 10, 2006. I did not undress or go to bed that night. At 4 AM, I wrote her obituary. About 6 AM, I wrote the following letter to our friends and relatives who were not notified by phone:

```
From: Jim Hammond

Date:   March 11, 2006 0630 AM

To:   Friends & Relatives

Subject:   Carey

Dear Friends & Relatives,

    At the end of a long period of
deep and totally peaceful sleep,
while I held her hand in mine, my
sweet angel Carey awoke in heaven at
11:39 PM last night, Friday, March
10. I am sustained and comforted by
my absolute certainty that she is
up there surrounded by her Heavenly
```

Father, a whole host of angels, her beloved mother and daddy, and by other loved ones who went before her. Nevertheless, after having been a part of my life and my very being for more than 66 years, the world is already a very lonely place for me without her.

She will be laid to rest in the Hammond family burial plot in beautiful Riverview Memorial Gardens here in Valdosta. What a perfect spot for my true southern lady's final resting place. Her grave site is in close view of the Withlacoochee River with its banks lined with beautiful old moss-draped water oak trees. One mile downstream, on the high banks of that same Withlacoochee River, is the beautiful home with its glorious view that she loved so dearly, where we lived for 18 happy years.

My whole family joins me in thanks and deep appreciation for your loving prayers and support.

Love and peace to each of you,

Jim

- - -

Returning home to our apartment without Carey was far from easy but life moves on. While I miss her terribly every day, good memories of her and our wonderful 66 years of marriage have almost erased my initial pain and despair. A combination of many things have made my adjustment to life without her and living alone much easier than I ever expected. By nature, I'm an optimistic person with few mood swings. My "highs" have always greatly exceeded my "lows" in terms of frequency, how long they last and their intensity.

When Carey died, I fully expected my high-low pattern to reverse itself. It did for a brief span following her death, but to my surprise, it very quickly righted itself and continued at its former level. Since I still miss her terribly, how can this be so? At first, when I pondered that question, there were momentary feelings of guilt and disloyalty, but I quickly dispelled them by reminding myself that she'd never want me to be depressed and down spirited. More importantly, I knew she was in a happy place where there's no pain or sorrow. Another major factor in my adjustment is that I stay extremely busy with things I love doing. Then there's my wonderful family who, led by Mac, closed ranks around me, included me in almost all their activities and made me feel loved. All these things came together to make things much, much easier for me than would have otherwise been possible. Very few people are blessed to the extent that I am.

Undergirding all the foregoing, was my almost subconscious application of my parents' recipe for a quick resolution of the inevitable tough times in life everyone encounters. That recipe or philosophy can be summed up in the words of an old song that went something like this—"Accentuate the positive, eliminate the negative and don't mess with Mr. In-between." From time to time during the worst of my ordeal, I found myself humming that tune under my breath. It helped. Thank you, Mother and Dad. This and all the philosophies my parents espoused, were deeply rooted in biblical principles and teachings. They consistently practiced what they preached and lived their lives in a way that set high moral and ethical standards for their children to follow.

    Listen up, you young teacher-parents. Although it may not appear so, young ears are listening to what you say and young eyes are watching what you do. Generally speaking, they are more likely to emulate what you do than what you say, if they differ. Don't send conflicting messages. Just practice what you preach. When children are raised up in the way they should go, they may stray from the course as young adults but they will find their way back. That's what the Bible says, and in my long life, I've never found a single Biblical teaching that was anything less then 100% correct.

    Well, that's my sermon for the day. Now it's time to write about mundane things such as my running career and my struggle this year to stay physically fit and fast on the track. But before I do, I'd like to say that writing this part of my story about Carey's death has been great therapy for me. She was one smart little lady. She knew exactly how to bring out the best in me. It was an ongoing process that I will sorely miss. I'm a far better person than I ever could have been without her. Without her, I pray that I won't backslide.

    My sport, track, has been likened to a jealous, high-maintenance mistress who tolerates no rivals. Thus far in 2006, there have been three serious rivals that have cost me dearly in terms of both speed and endurance. It was

What a Beautiful Sunset

not possible to train or exercise at all during the six weeks I spent at the hospital with Carey and several weeks following her death. Of course, all the stress involved also took its toll both mentally and physically.

Rival No. 2. I spent three weeks in May with Mac and Lynne at the beach in Destin, FL. There's something in that beach air that makes my flesh weak and willing. I always overindulge and eat far too much rich seafood and too many irresistible desserts, often two along with a big dinner—and no exercise to balance the scales. Oh I always do a little half-hearted jogging up and down the beach but it amounts to little or nothing.

Rival No. 3. An almost identical repeat of Rival No. 2 (except for a few more desserts) when I spent 10 days at the beach at our annual family vacation together over the 4th of July holiday.

Even though I exercised and trained really hard between these rivals, I regained none of my lost speed and endurance. Despite that, I won four gold medals on June 24 in the North Dakota—Minnesota Senior Olympics in Fargo, ND. I ran the 100-, 200-, 400- and 800-meter races. I'm proud of my medals but I won't be satisfied until I break a world record. I came very close in 2005 in Pittsburgh and now my best chance appears to be in 2009 when I'll be 95 and at the bottom of that age group (95 to 99). I'm not ruling out doing it in the 2007 National Senior Olympics in Louisville, KY, but it will be hard. I'll be 93 then and still in the 90–94 age group competing with all those young guys who just turned 90. With all this talk about breaking a world record, you must have correctly assumed that I plan

2006

to immediately get back on my year-round, five-days-a-week training program with no avoidable interruptions.

This is August 2, 2006. This insertion is not in date order due to an unexpected development in the past 10 days. Tomorrow we leave for Charlotte and my participation in the USA Track & Field National Masters Championship Meet. All my foregoing discourse about "rivals" was written right after our return from the beach on July 6. I must confess that the whole "rivals" thing was my poorly camouflaged attempt (subconscious, I hope) to prepare myself and my readers for a poor performance in Charlotte. In the course of my training, Mac often reminds me of a biblical truth; that is, "Quitters never win and winners never quit." In other words, you win if you never quit. Had he read my foregoing "rivals" discourse, he could have justifiably admonished me with, "Oh ye of little faith."

After weeks of very hard training without regaining any of the speed I had lost since this time a year ago, I had let a bit of negativity creep in and I had begun to wonder if I'd ever regain my former speed and endurance. One thing saved me. I didn't quit. I kept trying. A year ago, my 100-meter average in training sessions was 17.5. Until 10 days ago, my best this year was 20.9. Ten days ago, like a bolt out of the blue, I did it in 19.9. In every run since then, I have improved. Yesterday I did it in 18.2. That beats my time of 18.3 when I won a silver medal in the 2001 National Senior Olympics in Baton Rouge. The new world record is 17.8 and I'm getting close. Maybe in Charlotte. It's possible. A world record is in my future. The only way to lose is to quit and that will not happen.

What a Beautiful Sunset

From: Jim Hammond

To: Friends & Relatives

Subject: Another Boasting Opportunity—Four More Gold Medals

Date: July 14, 2006

Hi Friends & Relatives.

It's Jim Hammond's boasting time again. Ready to listen? If not, click on "delete" right now and I'll never know you did it.

On June 24, I won four gold medals (100-, 200-, 400- and 800-meter races) in Fargo, ND in the North Dakota—Minnesota Senior Olympic Games. It was my first time to compete in an 800-meter race and I wasn't sure I could even last to finish it, but I did and I won.

This track meet was totally different in the way it was handled. They made drastic changes in order to save time and their objective was accomplished in a big way.

Competition is held by age groups in 5-year increments (50-54, 55-59, etc.). I'm in the 90-94 age group—I'm 92. Normally, men and women don't run together and you run with your age group. This time, it was totally different. They herded us all together, irrespective of age or sex, and ran one heat right after another and all the events (100-, 200-, 400- and 800-meter races) were completed in less than two hours. About 30 minutes after the last race was run, the computers had sorted out and ranked the participants, by sex, in each age group and the winners were announced. Absolutely amazing!

We did in two hours what is normally spread out over at least three days. I was the only one in my age group to compete in all four events and now know why. There was hardly any recovery time between races and I was one tuckered out dude when I finished the last race, the 800-meter run. However, I experienced instant revival when the winners were announced and I walked away with four gold medals.

When I ran the 200-meter race, the man in the lane next to me and I ran neck and neck until I crossed the finish line half a step ahead of him. As we slowed to a stop, he asked in a very gruff voice, "How old are you?" "I'm 92," I answered. "Ninety-two! I'm 72 and I just ran my last race!" If he expected sympathy, he didn't get it. I was too busy feeling smug and a bit like superman at that moment.

When I was running the 400 meter race, I was leading the way at about the half-way point when a pretty little lady eased right past me with no apparent effort. It gave my manly pride a bit of a jolt when she glided across the finish line well ahead of me like a graceful gazelle. When I talked to her later, I learned that she was a recently widowed, 58-year-old mother of six and a three times grandmother, who held numerous running titles. She was from Minot, ND and she said there were many fast people there as they had to run fast to stay warm. At these track meets, I always meet one or more very interesting, vital and inspiring people who, like me, love to run and are totally dedicated to their sport.

This was my first visit to North Dakota and I found it interesting. The land is so flat and treeless it gave me a funny feeling.

Once outside the city, there's nothing higher than an ant hill to hide behind.

I'll always be grateful to a workout buddy who urged me to enter my very first race way back yonder when I was only 86 years old. It was the 100-meter run in the year of 2000 in the Georgia Golden Olympics. By some sort of miracle, I won a gold medal on my very first try. It set me on fire and I've been running ever since. That was the beginning of a wonderfully exciting running career that keeps on going and going and going and, hopefully, won't end anytime soon.

I'm looking forward to my next race that is coming up soon—the USA Track & Field Masters Championship Meet in Charlotte, NC on August 3 to 6. Wish me luck.

Thanks for letting me do what I enjoy most, am best at, and do most often—boastfully talk and write about my running accomplishments. Gotta go run now.

Tim

- - -

What a Beautiful Sunset

From: Jim Hammond

To: Friends & Relatives

Subject: My TV Coverage

Date: July 18, 2006

Hi Friends and Relatives,

   It's me again! I've been on television so many times this year (three times locally, three nationally) that it's gotten to be old hat. Oh yeah! If it keeps up, maybe Hollywood will send for me. Oh yeah again!

   Most recently, I was interviewed and photographed running and working out at my fitness center by a sports reporter, Ryan Kibbe, for local Channel 5 (ABC) and it was aired on their 6 PM newscast this past Friday and Saturday evenings. You can access Channel 5's website and view the broadcast by using the link shown in the message I am forwarding from my friend, Russ.

   I wouldn't enjoy life half as much as I do if I couldn't share all these little things (big to me) with my friends and relatives. Thanks.

Jim

- - -

2006

From: Jim Hammond

To: Friends & Relatives

Subject: Me on Good Morning America Show? Yes Indeed!

Date: July 18, 2006

Dear Friends & Relatives,

    Wonders never cease. Ryan Kibbe, Sports Reporter for our local ABC Channel 5, who did my piece that was aired last Friday and Saturday evenings, told me it would be sent to ABC Headquarters and they'd send it out to ABC stations across the country and it would be their option to air it or not do so. He did not indicate that it might be broadcast nationally. I almost went into shock when I received an e-mail letter from Amy, my Kentucky niece (I'm forwarding her letter), saying she had watched me on Good Morning America that morning.

    It would have been awesome to me had it been nothing more than an announcement on Good Morning America that I'd recently won four gold medals. But to be seen running, working out, and being interviewed on Good Morning America was for me overwhelming. That's real heady

What a Beautiful Sunset

stuff for this old, southern farm boy from Kentucky.

    I'm beginning to feel like a real celebrity and that's not good. I need Carey back down here right now to see that I keep my feet firmly on the ground where they belong. She had a wonderful way of doing it and never hesitated to do it anytime she saw my head beginning to grow.

Thanks for letting me share this minor miracle.

Jim

- - -

Forwarded Message

From: Amy Wood
Date: Tue, 18 Jul 2006 09:51:29 EDT
To: Jim Hammond
Subject: You Are Famous AGAIN

Uncle James,

    Wow, I'm working in one room with the television on this morning, in another room and all of a sudden I hear on Good Morning America, congratulations to Jim Hammond and I go running to see and hear more good things about you on television. How cool! We are all very proud of you.

Then I'm on the phone to my competition, Nancy Carol, and she again missed you on the tube. Surely my points are going up.

Think and pray for you daily.

Much love,

Amy

- - -

From: Jim Hammond

Date: Mon, 07 Aug 2006 11:44:12 -0500

To: Linda Aldridge

Subject: My Charlotte Waterloo

Hello Friends & Relatives,

Since my running career began six years ago, each time my ego grows and I began to feel unbeatable, something always comes along that brings me down and replants my feet firmly on the ground. The first time was at the 2003 National Senior Olympics in Norfolk, VA, and my disastrous fall. That was a lesson in humility I thought would last a lifetime, but not so. My once bruised and battered ego rebounded

What a Beautiful Sunset

quickly and completely when I broke two national records in Pittsburg in 2005. It continued to grow when I won four gold medals in Fargo in June 2006. It kept right on expanding with each new television appearance. Once again, I was beginning to feel invincible. My bubble was ready to explode by the time I arrived in Charlotte and that's exactly what it did.

    I was overdue for another stern humility lesson when I so confidently stepped off the plane onto the tarmac at the Charlotte, NC airport, late Thursday afternoon, August 3, into a heat index of 120 degrees.

    I was scheduled to run the 400-meter race at 3 PM the next day, Friday, and the 100-meter race at 1 PM Saturday. Due to the excessive heat and severe thunderstorms, no races were run Thursday afternoon or evening. After many delays, schedule changes and much confusion, it was finally settled that my age group would run the 400 at 12:30 PM Saturday and the 100 an hour and a half latter at 2 PM. With all the confusion and schedule changes, only two of us in my age group showed up for the 400-meter race.

After looking my lone competitor over, I thought to myself, *This will be a piece of cake.* Little did I know that my vain assumption had set me up big-time for a jarring come down. When I met that freshly turned 90-year-old from Vermont, I didn't dream that I was shaking the hand of my nemesis. If at that moment a clairvoyant flash had revealed that I would momentarily be eating his dust, I don't think I could have withstood the shock.

When the starting gun was fired, I got off to one of my better starts and was well ahead of him at the half-way mark. It's at that point that I always begin to tire and my pace slows down, but in the past, I've had enough steam left to cross the finish line first as everybody else slowed down too. But not this man from Vermont. He slowed down not at all and kept going at his same steady pace. At the 300-meter marker he passed me and kept gaining on me for the balance of that final 100 meters. Despite exerting my last ounce of energy, my feet moved no

What a Beautiful Sunset

faster and I had more meters left to go when he crossed the finish line than I'm willing to admit.

My running time was one minute and 51 seconds, which would be a winner in most races, but he did it in one minute and 39 seconds, one second shy of tying the one minute and 38 second world record. I have no excuses. He is a world-class runner and that's still in my future. He just beat me fair and square. He was a real gentleman about it—no gloating smirks, like the ones I try hard to repress when I win. For the record, he had just turned 90 and had broken all the records in his former 85 to 89 age group.

The 100-meter race was a different story as I should have won it hands down but didn't. The weakest part of my running game has always been my starts. I must be gun shy as I always jump and jerk when the gun is fired and the rest of the field is off the mark ahead of me before I collect myself and start running. But I always quickly catch up and lead the field all the way to the finish line. Except for an even worse start than usual, it worked very much the same this time. Although he was 10 strides or so ahead of me when I got started, I passed him very quickly and was leading him by at least 10 meters when I blasted across what I thought was the finish line and knew I had won the gold.

As I slowed down to a stop, there 10 feet ahead of me I could see the real finish line. Before I figured out what had happened and started running again, he had crossed the finish line. I was betrayed by my poor vision.

I will consider this meet a learning process and not let it sidetrack my ultimate goal—a world record. I learned several important lessons. First, I must find something to simulate the sound of a starting gun and practice hard on starts. Second, I must work harder on rebuilding my endurance to its former level for the 400-meter run. Never again in the 100-meter race will I mistake that first white line for the finish line.

This trip to Charlotte leaves me with no regrets for two reasons. I will become a better runner from the lessons I learned, but there's another more important reason why it was more than worthwhile. The prin-

What a Beautiful Sunset

cipal and almost only reason both Mac and I were interested in this meet was its location—Charlotte. We used the track meet as an excuse for a trip to Charlotte. Fifty-three years ago, when Mac was 10 years old, we moved to Charlotte and lived there three years (1953-1956). We bought a new house on a short street named Heathwood Road.

After the war, eight Charlotte veterans attend North Carolina State University (the Wolf Pack) on the GI Bill and lived in the same trailer park for married veterans all four years. When they graduated, all eight couples bought lots on Heathwood Road and built new homes. When we moved into our new home, we found ourselves in the midst of that N.C. State Wolf Pack and they took us in as part of the Pack. We became lifelong friends with almost all of them. Down through the years, we have kept in close contact with two of the couples, the Millers and the Hills, and through them, the rest of the group.

The prospect of revisiting our old neighborhood and getting together with some of our old neighbors was very exciting to both Mac and me. We were able to get in touch with only two couples—Jim and Frances Miller, who now live in nearby Gastonia, and Jean and Harvey Hill, who now live in Raleigh. Both couples agreed to come watch me run.

We were delighted when they showed up with Inez Arant. She and her husband (who died about two years ago) were our friends and neighbors and one of the eight couples in the old Heathwood Road Wolf Pack. Jim Miller also brought his youngest son, Chuck, who is a few years younger than Mac. After the races, we all had dinner together at our hotel and spent two wonderful hours reminiscing. I know Mac enjoyed the evening as much as I did. Like me, he has many sentimental memories of the three years we lived there.

If I had to choose between two gold medals and our time with our friends, the gold medals would be a distant second choice. I am sure Carey's spirit was right there with us enjoying each and every conversation. She dearly loved those wonderful friends as do Mac and I.

What a Beautiful Sunset

```
      Thanks, once again, for letting
me share my triumphs and my fail-
ures in such minute detail. I'd make
these epistles shorter if I knew
how.

Love,

Jim
```

- - -

A letter I recently received and my reply to it are reflective of a unique and very special friendship that I want to record and make a part of this story. When we moved to Valdosta, Georgia, in 1979, we chose for our family physician a highly recommended young doctor named John D. Anderson who had very recently begun his practice. He soon became our friend and beloved family doctor and remained so until we moved to Minnesota in 2001, 22 years later. We had little hope of finding a new family doctor with whom we could develop a comparable relationship. We should have trusted the Lord as he led us straight to Dr. John D. Dryer. Could the fact that they have the same first name and middle initial be a mere coincidence? Maybe so, but I like to think not. I liked him instantly and so did Carey.

Both of us responded to his genuinely warm, friendly manner, his obvious interest in us and his great sense of humor. Our personalities (his, Carey's, and mine) seemed to meld and a friendship above and beyond a normal patient-doctor relationship soon developed. Now, five years later, there's no one in the state of Minnesota whose friendship I value more highly. The fact that a medical journal recently ranked him as the Number One Family Physician in the

State of Minnesota is indicative of the kind of doctor he is. I take great pride and feel highly honored that he chose to be my good friend. Otherwise, I would not make the following letter a part of this story.

> Dear Mr. Hammond (Jim),
>
> I've been meaning to respond to all of your great press, but have been somewhat overwhelmed by it all. Since you have become such a national sports celebrity that must make me a doctor to the stars! Do you think that my good fortune (and great privilege and honor) to be your physician of record might get me some national T.V. coverage too? Then I could market myself as a boutique doctor caring for the rich and famous. The only problem with such a scenario is that I would have to make some significant wardrobe upgrades, and clothes-shopping is right up there with paper cuts in terms of enjoyable activities.
>
> Anyway, I'm just tickled that you did so well and, more importantly, that you are maintaining your sense of humor and zest for life. As I have said before, Carey is in no hurry to have you join her, and there are countless people who (for purely selfish reasons) want you around on

earth a lot longer. I count myself among those people, and have enjoyed sharing your humor and writing skills with my wife and two daughters.

Things are a bit frenetic here as both girls are participating in a big soccer tournament in Blaine all week, and we are trying to leave on our annual summer vacation to Traverse City, Michigan, as soon as the last game is finished. The summer is just flying by, and I always feel as if I'm not completing half of what I intend to do (witness the tardiness of this note).

Jim, I want you to know how special you are to me. Work has been extremely stressful for me for the last several years (for reasons not worth discussing), so I nearly accepted another position earlier this summer. However, when I sat down for my "pros and cons" analysis, the one "pro" that overwhelmed all other considerations is the pure joy I get from working with people such as you. Being a part of your life is at least as valuable to me as it is to you, and played a huge role in my decision to stay in my present position. I will be cutting my schedule somewhat starting in January, but know that there will always be time for you.

Sincerely,

John Dryer

- - -

Hi Dr. Dryer,

    I am always a bit reluctant to include you in my mass mailings because I know how very busy you always are and I do not want my long letters, filled with little more than a bunch of trivia and idle chatter, to become an added chore for you. Then, a reassuring letter always comes along that makes me glad I did.

    You and your letters have a wonderful way of making me feel like the nicest fellow in the world when I know I'm far from it. It's a great feeling so please don't stop.

    I'm sure all your patients would agree that the world would be a better and happier place if all doctors took the time to make their patients feel better about themselves as you so aptly do.

    It might be wise for you to slightly moderate your flatter-

What a Beautiful Sunset

ing remarks about me as I might begin to agree with you and that would be bad. You see, I no longer have Carey beside me to help me keep my feet on the ground. She had a wonderful way of doing exactly that each time she saw my head begin to grow. I'd like to share an example of how she did it with her wonderful wit and great sense of humor that made it so effective. I was the speaker at my 72nd high-school class reunion and I got a standing ovation when I finished. Later, when I told Mac about it, Carey said, "I was absolutely fascinated watching a distinguished-looking old gentleman with a white beard who was sitting on the front row. He slept and snored gently throughout your speech." She never had to pause and plan what to say and I secretly believe she made it up. But how could I possibly be mad or resentful over a funny remark like that? Mac would have enjoyed nothing more than being on hand every time she shot me down with one of her skillful but innocent appearing remarks.

Your friend and most vocal press agent,

Jim

- - -

Carey's Farewell Party January 27, 2006. It was Carey's last and best party. It was for our good Valdosta friends to meet our guests and help us celebrate our 60 year friendship with two very special friends—Sybil Mashburn of Atlanta and Gracelee Quillian of Charleston, SC. Pictured here are Carey, Sybil, me, and Gracelee.

Carey with one of her favorite bridge partners, Myrtis Howell.

What a Beautiful Sunset

More farewell party pictures. Marion Myddleton. Marion and her husband Jake, (now deceased), were our best Valdosta friends.

Our good friends left to right, Nancy Parrot, Dr. Bob Stump, and Dr. Jesse Parrot.

More farewell party pictures. Lee Bradley and Julia Best in the back. Georgia Thompson in front.

Judy DeMott on left—Vicki Ray on right.

What a Beautiful Sunset

Carey's casket with an incredibly beautiful blanket of spring flowers.

Sharon Stromley, a vocalist from Mac's church in Minneapolis, who has one of the most beautiful voices I've ever heard, flew down to sing one of Carey's favorite hymns, *We Shall Behold Him*.

2006

Taken Tuesday, March 14 after Carey's funeral. Jim, Hayden, Elayna, and Caroline.

Elayna, Caroline, Hayden, Jamey, and Jessey.

What a Beautiful Sunset

This photo was taken on April 5, 2006 at my 92nd birthday party. Happy Birthday kisses from two beauties—Kristin and Beckey.

Kristin showing me a picture she had just taken on her high-tech camera while Jim looks on.

2006

I'm opening presents while Kristin, LucyHart, Mac, John, Beckey, and Micheal watch.

My 35-year old baby grandson, John, sits in my lap while Elayna casually strolls by in the background.

What a Beautiful Sunset

John and his two children Jessey and Elayna at Easter.

Another Easter picture—John, Jessey, Elayna, and Beckey.

2006

This picture has an interesting story. The day Mac, Lynne, and I flew home, May 26, John, Beckey, and the two children went fishing on a charter boat. As John was reeling in a king mackerel, a barracuda ripped off the bottom half of it. As John reeled in the top half that was left, the barracuda came right to the side of the boat to get it and a deck hand harpooned it. The boat captain said that was the first time he'd ever heard of that being done. Jessey is holding the barracuda.

Both of my grandsons, Jim and John, two of my great grandsons, Jamey and Jessey, and my great granddaughter, Hayden, are very good athletes. One of my greatest joys is watching them compete and I am one of their most vocal fans. I love this picture of Jessey's near perfect pitching form that was taken when making a pitch in one of his games.

What a Beautiful Sunset

Jessey is sitting between Lynne and me after his conference winning game.

We left Minneapolis on June 28, 2006, for our annual family vacation together over the July 4th holiday at the beach in Destin, FL, and returned on July 6. Jim and his family are pictured here.

2006

LucyHart and her family.

John and his family.

What a Beautiful Sunset

All the adult male members of our family—John, Micheal, Jim, me, and Mac.

Kristin, Jamey, and Lynne

2006

I'm holding my youngest great granddaughter, sweet Elayna.

Mac and I at the USA Track & Field Meet in Charlotte on August 5, 2006.

What a Beautiful Sunset

Our good friends and former neighbors when we lived on Heathwood Road in Charlotte 53 years ago. Pictured left to right: Harvey Hill, Jean Hill, me, Mac, Inez Arant, Jim Miller, and Frances Miller.

Sybil Mashburn from Atlanta and Gracelee Quillian from Charleston flew to Minneapolis on September 5, 2006 and were my guests from Tuesday to Friday. They are the same two long-time friends (60 years) who visited us in Valdosta and for whom we gave a big party the day of Carey's fatal fall. I had something planned for them every minute of their visit and we had a wonderful time. On Thursday evening, Mac took the three of us and the rest of our family (17 in all) to dinner at P.F. Changs Restaurant in Maple Grove so everyone could meet my guests. This photo of Lynne, Sybil and me was taken there.

2006

Standing—Kristin, me, John and Gracelee. Seated—Lynne, Sybil, and Mac. At some point, Sybil asked Mac, "Since you are now an internationally famous minister, does it embarrass you to know that I changed your diapers 60 years ago when you lived in Charleston? I once baby-sat for you to give your parents a night out."

Conclusion

It must be God's plan for me to keep on living and running for several more years as He has continued to bless me with near-perfect health and more than my share of energy.

Since only God knows when I'll leave this world for my reunion in heaven with Carey, I do not plan to further update my story. However, I do hope Mac will make the final update for me after I join Carey.

He can make it an addendum to the "What a Beautiful Sunset" manuscript that I will leave with him – this for the benefit of any of my descendants who might be interested in an account of my life right on up to its very end. I like to think that my future will continue to hold enough excitement and adventure to keep me happy —maybe enough to fill a small booklet. Who knows?

To some who read my story, it might appear impossible for anyone to live a life with as few really tough times as the one I have pictured, and they might be right.

Everyone experiences trials, tribulations, disappointments and failures, and I'm sure I've had my share of each. A possible explanation of why my story reflects so few really bad times might be this: In my old age, my memories of my

What a Beautiful Sunset

bad times may have been almost totally obliterated by my memories of the good ones.

I learned early in my life to put my failures and bad times behind me, to dwell upon them as little as possible and to concentrate on continuing to press toward my goals. I was, for the most part, able to do so by keeping my thoughts and mind focused on the many good things with which the Lord has always blessed me. That could be why in my old age I can honestly look back on a long life with few memories of anything other than lots of love, joy, fun and happiness.

I hope you like my title for this story, *What a Beautiful Sunset*. I do. I loved beautiful sunsets long before they became, in my mind, analogous to the rapidly approaching end of my journey through life.

Back in the early 1970s, I purchased a waterfront lot on an island and built a beautiful home there simply because of the breathtaking beauty of the sunsets when viewed from that particular spot. It was on Point Manalapan, the southern tip of Hypoluxo Island in the middle of Lake Worth with Palm Beach to the east and Lantana, Florida to the west. We chose the west side of the island. When the sun set behind a group of stately royal palm trees on the opposite shore, it painted a patch of low-hanging clouds with a myriad of rainbow colors and cast across the broad expanse of water a bright, fiery, red-gold path that led straight to where each of us sat on our patio. It was much like the one pictured on the front cover of this book. It would be hard for any believer to witness such a spectacular display of natural beauty without feeling the presence of God.

As I rapidly approach the inevitable end of my long life on planet Earth, I become more and more sentimental about

Conclusion

my family and I think more frequently about my immortality. It pleases me to think that my two books, *A Kentucky Kernel & His Folks* and *What a Beautiful Sunset*, are my legacy for my family, and it is my implausible hope that they will be passed on down to one or more of my descendants in each succeeding generation, thereby assuring my immortality. At this late stage in my life, the sky seems to be the limit in my dreams.

THE END

This photo, among many others, was taken of me in March 2007 by internationally famous, Pulitzer prize-winning photographer, Rick Rickman. He was sent here by *Eldr Magazine*. They are doing a feature story on me in the June 2007 introductory issue of their new magazine. While another photo was selected for the front cover, this one is far and away my favorite for its beauty from a purely artistic viewpoint. I think it's a prime example of why he's famous and why he's considered a true master at his craft.